25 *best* planting PLANS

25 *best* planting PLANS

Noël Kingsbury

Additional research by Sharron Long

WARD LOCK

A WARD LOCK BOOK

First published in the UK 1996 as *The Ultimate Planting Guide*
This edition first published 1999
by Ward Lock
Wellington House
125 Strand
LONDON
WC2R OBB

A Cassell Imprint

Distributed in the United States
by Sterling Publishing Co., Inc.
387 Park Avenue South, New York, NY 10016-8810

A British Library Cataloguing in Publication Data block for this book may
be obtained from the British Library.

ISBN 0 7063 7789 3

Designed by Grahame Dudley Associates
Cover artwork by Gill Tomblin

Printed and bound in Spain by Graficromo S.A., Cordoba

Page 1: A campanula and a diascia make an attractive, easy
combination for a container – and one which is more subtle than traditional
pelargoniums and petunias.

Page 2: A selection of strong colours is skilfully blended
to form an harmonious whole, the effect enhanced by the glaucous foliage
of a mertensia.

CONTENTS

INTRODUCTION

WHERE DO YOU START when you want to plant up your garden? It can seem a bewildering business. First comes the problem of what plants to choose. Books are full of attractive pictures but unattractive Latin names, other people's gardens are always filled with plants lovely to look at but difficult to find, and your garden centre is filled with so many unfamiliar things that you can never find what you like. Then, having decided on some plants, the next problem is putting them all together: will they grow well next to each other, and will the combination look good?

This book aims to guide you through the jungle of plant combinations – the art of finding plants and styles that you like, that will look good in your garden, and that will grow successfully.

The planting plans in this book present numerous inspirational ideas for you to copy or adapt to suit your own garden. There are plans for family gardens that will take three dogs and a toddler in their stride, for low-maintenance gardens designed for those who want to sit and enjoy, rather than dig, and plans for gardens with an exotic theme for those who would rather be somewhere else altogether. There are designs for so-called 'difficult' sites, such as dry areas, shade and boggy spots, although these should be thought of as places of potential, special places where a different range of plants may grow. There are designs for town gardens, cottage gardens, spring and autumn gardens – in short, a garden for every place, every desire. All are designed to function for many years, whether planted as suggested or used as a springboard for your own ideas.

If you are thinking of creating a new garden or replanting part of an existing one, leaf through the planting plans until you find one that appeals to you and that is suitable for your garden. Reflect on your favourite plants. What do they have in common? It may be that they all have brightly coloured flowers, or your preference may be to do with habit of growth: neat, cushion-shaped plants may appeal, or the elegant, arching grace of a plant may be more your style. Take time to consider all these factors, because knowing what you like is a fundamental part of creating anything.

Like much of life, gardening is the art of compromise, of getting the balance right between what you want and what is possible to grow. You also need to consider the shape and design of your garden, and select a planting plan which will not only look good and keep you and your vision happy, but which will keep your plants healthy. This book, with its plan for every garden, and every spot in that garden, aims to help you to have the garden you have always dreamed of, without any nightmares.

Opposite: Hosta sieboldiana *var.* elegans *and* Polystichum setiferum *will form an attractive combination all summer long in a shady or moist spot.*

GARDEN TYPES
AND STYLES

THE MOST FUNDAMENTAL questions to do with planting and design are practical ones. What is the garden going to be for? Is it primarily for show, creating a nice view from the house, or is it to be enjoyed on a more active basis? Will it be used for entertaining, barbecues and parties? Do you have small children, or (even worse for plants) large ones, or perhaps grandchildren? Do you have pets? Do you want to grow only ornamental plants, or would you like fruit and vegetables as well? Do you have special interests – alpines or roses, for example?

In most cases, a garden has to fulfil several functions, so compromises are necessary. The traditional format of lawn with borders allows space for entertaining and children's play, but also for growing attractive plants or vegetables. Conversely, those who are more interested in gardening for its own sake should perhaps consider reducing the size of the lawn or getting rid of it entirely. It is perfectly possible to plant right across a garden, with narrow paths that give access to all areas, but which are more or less invisible from the distance, creating an illusion of continuous planting.

GARDENS FOR CHILDREN

Whatever else you may want to do with a garden, if you have young children they will end up dictating the basic framework. The garden must be a safe place for them, so there should be no nasty prickles or thorns, or plants that look attractive to play with or eat but that are poisonous. However, every gardener with a family knows that the children end up doing more damage to the garden than vice versa. Their activities often end up with balls and toys being lost in borders, followed by expeditions to find them, and plantings provide inviting places to play hide-and-seek or build dens.

First and foremost, children need a lawn, and the more space they have, the less damage there is likely to be around it. If the garden is big enough, you should think about planting specifically for children's games, with bushes to hide in and narrow, winding paths that encourage the imagination. It helps to think about things at their height – a number of shrubs at adult head-height can become an exciting jungle for children. Further suggestions for a family garden are given on pages 62–3

Gardens for families need to be flexible, with plenty of space
provided for children to play, and places for entertaining as
well as for relaxation.

GARDENS FOR ENTERTAINING

Gardens that are used for entertaining need plenty of lawn space for guests to move around and in which to set up barbecues or discotheques. Around the grass you will need something for guests to look at other than the fence or the neighbour's plot. A well-planted garden will not only provide a pleasant environment for entertaining but will also furnish plenty of talking points, especially if you have included some unusual plants. Planting that looks its best when you do most of your entertaining (usually summer) is important, as is scent. Most fragrant plants come into their own in the evening, which is very convenient, and can add immeasurably to a romantic party atmosphere. Plants in containers are also a good idea for those who entertain often, because they can be put on show or hidden away depending on how good they are looking.

GARDENS FOR SHOW

Most gardeners want their gardens to look good for as long as possible, to create a good impression in the neighbourhood or simply as an attractive view from the windows – or all three. It is not too difficult to bring together a selection of plants that look attractive and interesting for much of the year, but creating space to plant them in is perhaps more of a challenge.

If a constantly changing array of flowers, fruit and foliage is your priority, perhaps this is another time to challenge the supremacy of the lawn. If it is not actually going to be used, especially in a small front garden, why not dig it up and plant something more interesting instead? How about extending the border to cover the whole of the area, with narrow paths criss-crossing it? The traditional cottage garden is a bit like this (see pages 76–8), but there is no reason why any border theme cannot be developed in this way: take a look at the very formal garden based on paths, gravel and small clipped hedges on pages 60–61, or the opposite extreme of drifts of colourful perennials and grasses on pages 86–7.

GARDENS FOR WILDLIFE

Gardeners who want to cater for wildlife will put a low priority on lawns, preferring wildflower meadows along with lots of shrubs and undergrowth. Making a successful nature reserve in your garden means providing both food sources and safe places for birds, amphibians and insects to breed. At the same time, the garden needs to be attractive and also open enough for you to be able to see and appreciate the wildlife it attracts, preferably from the house.

Diversity is the key to encouraging a wide variety of wildlife, so you will need to include different habitats and numerous food sources – such as thick grass, shrubs, a pool and wetland – in the garden. Birds in particular appreciate trees and shrubs at a variety of heights and thick shrubbery, which makes for safe nesting. Grass or wildflower meadows provide habitats for different species of insects, which in turn provide food for insectivorous birds. A good seasonal spread of flowering plants will supply nectar for insects both early and late in the year. Finally, a range of shrubs with berries will keep the birds interested for much of the winter. Ideas on the nitty gritty of wildlife gardening and on establishing a suitable garden can be found on pages 66–9.

GARDENS FOR FOOD

Apart from the lawn, the main practically orientated parts of the garden will be areas for growing fruit, vegetables and herbs. Long relegated to the rear of the plot, as if the working garden were somehow shameful, it is time to consider how edible plants can be integrated with the rest of the garden. Certain practical or aesthetic considerations may dictate their being kept separate – proximity to the compost heap and the undeniable tattiness of brussel sprouts in winter are two that come to mind – but think how beautiful red-tinged oakleaf lettuces, bulging yellow squashes and feathery carrot tops can be.

It should go without saying that herbs need to be near the kitchen door, since no cook wants to

Colourful phlox, achilleas and ornamental cabbages contribute
to a relaxed cottage-garden atmosphere.

traipse through the garden in a force-nine gale searching for a sprig of mint. Many herbs are quite decorative as well, so there is no problem in fitting them into borders or other plantings. Alternatively, a garden plan based on herbs is given on pages 48–9.

GARDENS FOR PLANTS

Of course the garden will have plants in it, but some gardeners are lovers of plants above all else. These people are enthusiasts and actually collect plants, so they will need need a garden that suits their hobby, designed primarily to be able to fit in lots of new acquisitions. In my experience, these gardeners often live with a partner who is interested in more mundane considerations, such as whether the garden looks nice, and such 'plantsman' gardeners must learn the art of compromise in order to accommodate their collections to the other uses of the garden. The best solution is to ensure that all members of the family are happy with a basic framework consisting of lawns, paths, a place for herbs and salad vegetables and some attractive shrubs and perennials. The enthusiast can then fill in the gaps, or perhaps have a corner of his or her own. We will look in more detail at the enthusiast gardener on page 18.

AMBIENCE

Having thought about what the garden is for, let us now discuss some aesthetic factors and think about how you want your garden to look. The architecture of your house or neighbourhood or the surrounding countryside can seem almost to dictate a certain style: 'olde worlde' charm or pastoral scenery might suggest cottage gardens full of colourful scented flowers tumbling between old-fashioned roses, or perhaps something a little more formal, yet still capturing the essence of times gone by, using clipped hedges, rectangular pools and precisely ordered planting.

But do old buildings *have* to be surrounded by this kind of planting? Isn't it a bit unoriginal, boring even, for everyone in a pretty village to have a garden that looks like something out of a historical romance? I have a friend in a picture-postcard, half-timbered house, which used to have a classically formal little garden but she has ripped it up and replaced it with an asymmetrical series of hedges delineating rectangular beds, rather like a Mondrian painting, to create an uncompromisingly modernist effect. Yet the garden remains in keeping with its surroundings, as the hedges and border plants used here are much the same as those in the rest of the garden and are typical of the cottage-inspired style – the content is the same, only the form is different.

Often gardeners are not daring enough. Dramatic contrasts between old and new can work surprisingly well; what is important to avoid is cliché. Anything that looks suburban, for instance, can bring a whole set of inappropriate associations to mind in a country setting, while the ubiquitous tall hedge of leyland cypress (x *Cupressocyparis leylandii*) can often spoil a picturesque or natural landscape.

Just as with interior design, it is possible to create all kinds of different ambiences in the garden using both plants and objects. Some remind us instantly of a particular place or environment: bamboo – the Far East; a classical urn – Italy; large-leaved plants – the jungle; grey foliage – dry, sunny hillsides in Spain or California. Using these plants in a garden can create a very powerful sense of place. The problem is that they have such strong associations that it can be difficult to use them in other ways: bamboo could look lovely next to a thatched cottage, but when you are trying to create a traditional English garden it is like going on holiday with the wrong guidebook.

The creation of a distinct ambience is most successful when it is carried out in an enclosed garden or corner, or in surroundings to which it is appropriate. An example of the former might be a tiny courtyard, where a Japanese feel is often very successful, and of the latter a pastoral landscape, where a European-style formal garden is very much in keeping.

Creating a distinctive ambience is a challenge, but the result is most rewarding if it works, especially when carried out in cramped and hostile surroundings, such as a city backyard or roof garden with tenements and factories as neighbours. Part of the trick is to block out eyesores with creeper-covered trellis, trees or other plantings, but the real magic lies in creating a garden that so holds the attention that the eye is not tempted to stray beyond. Some of the more distinct ambiences are

There are few sights more satisfying than rows of vegetables, for at the end of the day we know we can eat them! Sweet peas add a touch of colour to this productive patch.

dealt with on pages 14–18, while on pages 22–3 consideration is given to the possibilities of creating gardens in confined urban environments.

HOW MUCH EFFORT?

In thinking about the uses of the garden, we must not neglect the very act of gardening itself – some people actually enjoy it for its own sake! A low-maintenance garden may be what many of us

want, but not everyone: a lot of people find gardening therapeutic and a relaxing and healthy break from office or indoor work. Others seek the company of plants and flowers, to have nature humming and pulsing around them. Choosing the right level of maintenance is very important for your enjoyment of the garden, and you will need to strike the correct balance between, on the one hand, being faced with too many chores to carry out, and, on the other having too little to do.

When planning a garden or even just a new planting, it is important to consider at the outset how much time and effort it will involve. This depends partly on the plants used and partly on the kind of planting. Some plants are undeniably high maintenance in any setting – hybrid tea roses, for example, always require annual pruning. Others need a lot of attention only in some contexts: for example, many of the taller, late-flowering herbaceous plants, such as rudbeckias and asters, have a reputation for being hard work since they need feeding, staking and tying up, cutting back in the winter and dividing every other year, but this is true only if you are growing them in the conventional way. In the traditional herbaceous border, plants are grown in separate clumps and fed well, resulting in much taller and weaker growth than they would make in the wild. The modern way of growing them – in poorer soil, blended with each other and with ornamental grasses – means that they stand up better, with no need for support. The style of planting can have considerable impact on how plants actually grow.

Some planting styles also require higher standards of maintenance if they are to appear attractive and well cared for. Everyone will look askance at the odd weed in a formal bedding scheme, for example, but it would be less likely to offend the eye in a cottage-garden border, and would not even be noticed in a wildflower meadow.

In considering maintenance, you will need to think not only about the time involved but also about the kind of work – a little gentle weeding is a world away from pushing around huge piles of manure in a wheelbarrow.

LOW AND HIGH MAINTENANCE

Here we consider different garden styles and how much work they involve, starting with the style that requires the hardest work and ending with the one that needs the least, together with some indication of the tasks required.

FORMAL BEDDING

This is the style beloved of parks the world over, and it is characterized by geometric arrangements of brightly coloured annuals. You either love it or hate it. Usually I hate it, but sometimes it is so well done and artistic you have to admire the achievement. France and Romania are the two countries that do it to its excessive best, to the point of using wire frameworks to support three-dimensional plant sculptures, but whatever you feel about it there is no denying that bedding out is hard work. Everything has to be planted out every year, kept rigorously weeded and watered often, and then dug up in the autumn. The ground has either to be kept bare all winter or planted up with winter bedding, such as bulbs and pansies. Replacing plants every year is expensive if they are purchased from a garden centre or nursery, and to do it yourself

*Formality and informality combined make a powerful statement. The standards here are a species of privet (*Ligustrum*) and* crataegus.

requires a greenhouse, a propagator and lots of time.

There is no doubt, however, that this is the style that really creates front-garden impact, and that the best practitioners of the art are usually retired people with plenty of time.

FRUIT AND VEGETABLES

These really are as much hard work as bedding out, but at least you can eat the results and you don't have to worry so much about the beds looking spick and span. If you are at all serious about being self-sufficient you will nearly always have something to do – sowing, planting out, weeding, harvesting, watering, and digging in or spreading compost. Many people prefer to grow just a few vegetables, perhaps some salad specialities such as lettuce and spring onions that are best eaten as fresh as possible, or particular varieties that are difficult to buy in the shops, such as old-fashioned and tasty tomatoes.

ROSE BEDS

Another favourite of public parks, the traditional rose bed is usually planted with varieties that need meticulous pruning every year, and nothing else is allowed to grow around them. Weeding is then a fairly constant task, as there is nothing that weeds like more than bare ground. Roses are prone to all sorts of fungal diseases that might not matter so much in a more casual setting but tend to be very noticeable in a formal one like this, so regular spraying throughout the summer is often needed. I find this the most unsatisfactory method of growing roses, as on their own they always strike me as garish in appearance, and they look dreadfully forlorn in winter.

TRADITIONAL HERBACEOUS BORDERS

Like the old-style rose bed, the traditional herbaceous border, planted entirely with perennials in discrete clumps, demands a lot of attention. The plants require an annual cut-back in winter, and until they are back in full growth again the following summer the gaps between them will need weeding, while staking and tying the taller plants, such as delphiniums and asters, to stop them flopping about in the wind and rain are time-consuming and fiddly exercises. Having said all this,

The popular cottage-garden style depends for its success on a carefree assortment of flowers, preferably in soft colours.

however, a well-planted herbaceous border is a magnificent sight in late summer and autumn, and for many dedicated gardeners it is worth all the trouble.

FORMAL GARDENS

In this context, 'formal gardens' means the use of clipped evergreens like yew (*Taxus* species) and box (*Buxus* species) in the form of hedges and topiary. This style is not as labour intensive as you might think, unless, of course, you are the fortunate purchaser of a property where there are already sizeable hedges. Although they will need clipping only once a year, this is quite a skilled operation.

MIXED BORDERS

Very much the style of the last few decades, the mixed border combines shrubs, perennials, bulbs and annuals to give a succession of colour and interest through the year. Planting is usually fairly tight, so weeds do not get too much of a chance to insinuate themselves, but the level of maintenance involved does depend very much on the plants that are used.

COTTAGE GARDENS

A style that has also become very popular since the 1950s, the cottage garden is perhaps a middle-class fantasy of how poor country people used to garden, but it is undeniably attractive and fairly low in maintenance needs. Indeed, a certain untidiness is part of the ambience, and self-sowing is *de rigeur*. The idea is to mix 'traditional' perennials, annuals, fruit, vegetables and herbs together in an attractive jumble of soft colours and sweet fragrances. The tight planting characteristic of this style keeps weeds out, but the emphasis on herbaceous plants does mean that at least one good annual clearout of dead vegetation is vital if it is not to look distinctly abandoned. This style is ideal for those who like a little pottering, with occasional weeding, staking and seed sowing, but who do not fancy the dedication needed for the traditional herbaceous border.

LAWNS

Grass is the conventional ground-cover plant for large areas but, as any of us with anything larger than a postage stamp of grass well know, lawns can be very time consuming. All grass really needs is regular cutting throughout the summer, but a lawn to be proud of requires far more: feeding, aeration, weed control, mowing and watering can consume whole weekends of your time.

Indeed, in some areas where there are statutory limits on water use, the maintenance of a conventional verdant lawn may be virtually impossible. I think it is time to look critically at the large expanses of green that cover so much of our gardens and to consider alternatives, ones that involve reduced use of precious natural resources and less work and that, let's be honest, look more interesting.

WILDFLOWER MEADOWS AND OTHER 'NATURAL' PLANTINGS

Very much the style of the moment, 'wild' plantings are, in theory, low maintenance. The idea is to establish a community of plants that will coexist happily and flourish because they are suited to the prevailing conditions. Plant selection is therefore important, and so is careful attention while the planting is becoming established. Once this phase is past, maintenance can be reduced to a minimum, a once-a-year cut being all that is needed. Even if you are a conventionally tidy-minded gardener, there is no denying the usefulness of wild gardens in out-of-the-way or difficult-to-get-to corners.

SHRUBS AND GROUND COVER

Perhaps given a bad name by unimaginative 'landscaping' around supermarkets and motorway junctions, the use of shrubs and low-growing evergreen ground covers is a highly effective way of sealing the ground against weeds and providing some interest all year round. The species chosen should mostly be evergreens and, of course, ones that do not require fancy pruning regimes. This does not have to mean boring berberis – the range of possible species is actually very wide, but it has to be said that the emphasis on evergreens can make for monotony after a few years, especially in shady areas. Once established, however, the attention these plants need is absolutely minimal.

For open sites, a popular and very colourful variant on this theme is the combination of dwarf conifers and heathers, where maintenance is restricted to cutting back every few years.

THE ENTHUSIAST'S GARDEN

Enthusiasts are those gardeners who have a passion for growing one particular kind of plant. Their hobby could be cultivating alpines, growing vegetables or flowers for competitive showing, or just taking an interest in one plant group, such as hardy cyclamen, bamboos or old-fashioned roses.

Some of these pursuits, such as the growing of prize vegetables, are visually difficult to fit into the rest of the garden and are perhaps best given their own special area, screened off from the main part. Others can make a major contribution, but their place needs to be considered carefully if the garden is not to become simply a collection of plants. A specialist rhododendron display, for example, can be stunning for two months of the year, but jolly dull for the other ten, so subsidiary plantings should be made to create colour and interest for the rest of the year, with bulbs to make a splash in the spring and small groups of late-flowering perennials, such as golden rods *(Solidago* species) and rudbeckias, to provide colour later on.

Specialist gardening sometimes involves greenhouses, cold frames, rock gardens or raised beds. In my experience, these are often an eyesore, with no thought given to how they might fit in with the rest of the garden. However, there is no reason why this should be the case: these items are not especially attractive, but their effect can be softened by planting low shrubs or perennials around the base of greenhouses and frames, and making raised beds and rock gardens that follow the contours of the ground or echo the lines of other garden features, such as borders or paths.

COLLECTABLE PLANTS

Cacti and succulents

You either love them or hate them – especially cacti. Needing to overwinter indoors in many areas, cacti and succulents benefit greatly from standing outside in the summer, opening up all sorts of exciting bedding-out possibilities. Ideally, the plants should be planted out in their pots, up to their necks in a very free-draining material such as sand, gravel or an open soil.

Flowers for show

Flowers for showing can usually be integrated quite well into borders with other plants. They will need constant attention, though, so good access is vital. This can be achieved by growing them in narrow borders or in beds cross by paths. The same applies to plants grown to produce flowers for cutting.

Alpines

Alpines are pretty addictive, especially for those whose gardening style is cramped by a tiny garden or through disability. The plants vary greatly in their tolerance of winter weather: some will survive outside in raised beds, in containers such as sink gardens, or growing on lumps of tufa rock; others need protection from winter wet and should be covered with sheets of glass or placed in a cold frame during wet weather.

Vegetables

Even if vegetables are grown separately from other plants, the vegetable garden can still be made attractive with the addition of occasional herbs and flowers. Certain flowers, such as English marigolds (*Calendula officinalis*), also act as 'companion plants' to vegetables, discouraging pests and encouraging bees. Vegetable areas can be screened off from the rest of the garden by hedges, or by trellis covered with climbers.

Herbs

Like vegetables and flowers for cutting, herbs need good access and so should never be too far from a path. Many herbs, both culinary and medicinal, are reasonably decorative plants, but the area can be made more attractive with the addition of some purely ornamental plants. Low box hedges are a traditional feature of herb gardens but should not be allowed to get too big, as the roots are quite greedy.

A PLANT FOR EVERY PLACE

FEW OF US START OFF with a blank space to plant up from scratch. When we move into a new house we usually find that a basic structure of beds and borders has already been established in the garden. However, there is no need to accept what is there; one of the keys to good garden design is an ability to see new possibilities among pre-existing structures.

The vast majority of plants in gardens are grown in company with others, in borders that hug the boundary – be it fence, hedge or wall – or the side of the house, or in beds, such as island beds. The idea of the traditional border or bed may, however, be expanded to encompass a much wider stretch – perhaps even the whole garden, thus doing away with grass entirely.

Different countries tend to have different traditions about where planting takes place; the Americans have open gardens without boundaries and 'foundation planting' around the house, the British mostly have lawns with borders along the boundaries, while the Dutch generally have small front gardens that tend to be planted up completely. Being adventurous in terms of planting and garden design may mean breaking with a national tradition.

SPECIMEN PLANTS

These are plants – usually trees but often shrubs or even particularly statuesque perennials – that stand on their own, usually in grass. They can make all the difference to a space, especially an open one, but they need to be in proportion to the house and the area they occupy: many is the cedar that not only overshadows the neighbour's garden but also overpowers the house.

A good specimen plant is well shaped above all else, its form being apparent and pleasing at all times of the year. A specimen tree should have more than one string to its bow and attractive flowers or autumn colour are bonuses. Vast lawns may support the extravagantly asymmetrical tiered branches of a cedar of Lebanon (*Cedrus libani*), but most of us only have space for something much smaller. Trees that make good specimens for small gardens are generally those with upward-sweeping branches, like the ornamental apple *Malus tschonoskii*.

Fine architectural perennials may also be used as specimen plants, the pampas grass (*Cortaderia selloana*) being the most commonly seen example. An alternative would be to use any of the miscanthus grasses, which are still imposing but which are more delicate. There is also plenty of

Annual lavatera and cosmos frame and complement – but do not overwhelm – a garden statue.

APPROACHES TO PLANTING

A Open front lawns in suburban settings may require only one specimen tree, the majority of the planting being around the house. Be adventurous, and don't restrict yourself to traditional evergreens – try some shrubs that will benefit from the protection of the wall, such as ceanothus. Use perennials, bulbs and annuals to enliven the border in front of the shrubs.

B A variation on the open suburban theme is to have island beds in the lawn, in this case incorporating a small specimen tree. It is important that the size of the beds is in proportion to the area of lawn: too often beds are made too small and look rather ridiculous.

C Where a garden has well-defined boundaries, the traditional approach is for the borders to follow them, with a lawn in the middle and maybe a specimen tree or shrub in the lawn. This makes for shallow borders, ideal for traditional bedding plants and annuals, or plants that need either constant attention or easy access, such as cut flowers, herbs or vegetables. It also maximizes the lawn area.

D Borders around the outside of the garden can be made deeper to allow more plants to be grown. This approach can be taken in any plot; it helps to create a sense of privacy in a garden with an open aspect, but is especially appropriate and successful in gardens which are already surrounded by a high fence or wall. This style suits those who want a romantic retreat or who like a varied collection of plants.

E In this garden, the lawn has been dispensed with entirely and the space given over to low-growing perennials and shrubs, around which paths meander. With careful selection of low-maintenance plants this kind of planting can involve less work than a lawn. It is ideal for those who wish to grow a wide variety of plants, would like to incorporate a naturalistic pond or want to create a garden for wildlife.

A

B

scope for the imaginative use of other large perennials, such as the imposing silvery cardoon plant (*Cynara cardunculus*) or the giant hogweed (*Heracleum mantegazzianum*) – note that the latter can give a nasty rash to some people. One potential advantage of using herbaceous perennials as specimen plants is that they are seasonal rather than permanent features of the garden.

BORDERS

If a plant is not grown on its own as a specimen, it is usually grown in a border. 'Border' means an edge, and that is just what most garden plantings are – a strip along a boundary, fence, hedge or wall. It seems to be a fundamental part of human nature to want to adorn those places where the vertical meets the horizontal. It is as if we have a deep need to fill the corner, to round it off with greenery.

Such places do offer a lot to the gardener – a vertical surface for climbers and a backdrop for taller perennials and shrubs, which in turn set the stage for smaller perennials, bulbs and annuals, and the exploitation of all the possibilities on offer is part of what makes an adventurous gardener. Borders are also convenient places for planting, which will not get in the way of whatever takes up the body of the garden, tea parties, ball games or the view from the house, but this convenience should not blind us to the scope offered by planting elsewhere in the body of the garden.

Borders have gone through many incarnations in the history of gardening. From tree and shrub borders on large estates and the grand herbaceous border of the earlier part of this century, today the 'mixed' border – a pragmatic blend of shrubs, perennials, annuals and climbers, and perhaps the odd vegetable or fruit bush – reigns supreme.

Borders are relatively easy to plant. You only have to see one side of a plant, and you can hide the unattractive 'bare legs' that many flowering perennials or shrubs develop behind shorter plants.

PLANTING AROUND FEATURES

Most gardens have more to them than plants. There may be a patio or terrace, a summerhouse, statues or other garden ornaments. All these features need to be integrated into the garden, so that they become a relevant part of it, and this can be done

with appropriate planting. On the other hand, there are 'features' that one might want to do without – that factory across the road, for example – and where screening will be needed (see page 33).

Desirable garden features should not be hidden, or put in the shade, by something that steals all the attention. Statues, sundials or other free-standing ornaments can be enhanced subtly around the base with planting, which should be neutral in tone but nevertheless attractive. Most sculpture needs to be unencumbered to be appreciated, but I have seen works that benefit from being partially hidden, seen behind greenery or at the back of a border.

Luxuriant and striking foliage is often a feature of waterside planting. The pale orange highlight is provided by Euphorbia griffithii, *which will thrive in many different soils.*

Some ornaments require a context that plants can help to provide; an oriental piece, for example, may well benefit from the company of bamboo or other plants associated with the East. A classical sculpture or urn likewise needs a summer planting of pelargoniums and a setting involving some formal clipped yew or box.

Sitting places, such as summerhouses and terraces, are crucial. Here people linger and have time to appreciate the garden, but also to notice if things are not quite right. Plenty of colour and interest are essential for the season during which the area will be used and this is why bedding and

patio plants are so popular, as they generally flower all summer long.

Scent is important too, and not only scented flowers but aromatic foliage as well. This can create quite a talking point as guests try the different leaves in turn. The scented-leaved pelargoniums are invaluable on this account, and eminently collectable. Such a situation is also ideal for plants that are not fully hardy, including all sorts of conservatory and greenhouse exotica that are brought out for the frost-free months such as daturas, with their fabulously scented trumpets, oleanders, bougainvilleas, palms and cacti.

PLANTING AROUND WATER

Small ponds are very popular, but to be effective they need to be sited carefully to avoid appearing out of place. They look best when treated with either total formality or total informality – nothing inbetween ever seems to work. A formal pool, rectangular in shape and with paved surrounds, is uncompromisingly formal and is therefore accepted as such, but an informal pond has to look as if it could be natural to work at all visually. No pool should ever be made on a slope: they just do not occur like that in nature and always look absurd.

Formal pools should have only sparse planting around them – perhaps some architectural plants with grand foliage (*Hosta sieboldiana* is rightly a classic). Containers can also be used to give a Mediterranean feel. Planting in the pool itself should be restricted to a few water lilies (*Nymphaea* and *Nuphar* species) and perhaps an iris at the edge; anything more and it will begin to look cluttered.

An informal pool should not have the edge, let alone the liner, showing at all. Lush and leafy plants leaning over the edge and marginals such as irises reaching out of the water will help to give it a natural feel, blending the pool with the rest of the garden. Ideally, there should be a ledge at the side of the pool where moisture-loving plants can be grown, and the whole should be backed by tall perennials, grasses or shrubs and trees like willows (*Salix* species), which we automatically associate with the waterside. If there is no ledge for marginal planting, select some large perennials that will look reasonably lush but that thrive in normal soil – the rhubarbs (*Rheum* species) are a good example.

Most water plants grow large and lush and can overwhelm a small pool, necessitating constant cutting back and dredging, which can disrupt pondlife. It is essential that plants are chosen that suit the size of the pool: less vigorous relatives of classic water plants are available, including pygmy water lilies and dwarf reedmace (*Typha minima*).

WATERSIDE VEGETATION, FROM DRY LAND TO OPEN WATER

1 Moisture-loving plants create the right context for a pool and most will grow well enough in ordinary garden conditions. Examples include *Lythrum salicaria*, *Iris sibirica*, *Lobelia cardinalis* and *Primula japonica*.

2 Marginal plants for wet soil and shallow water should be planted in soil on a ledge of the pond liner. Examples include *Iris pseudacorus*, *Butomus umbellatus* and *Acorus gramineus*.

3 Submerged aquatics such as *Myriophyllum spicatum* may not contribute much to the ornamental character of the pond, but they benefit pond life and help to suppress algae.

4 Water lilies (*Nymphaea* and *Nuphar* species) grow in soil at the base of the pond, producing their leaves and flowers at the surface. Nearly all these plants need sun in order to flower.

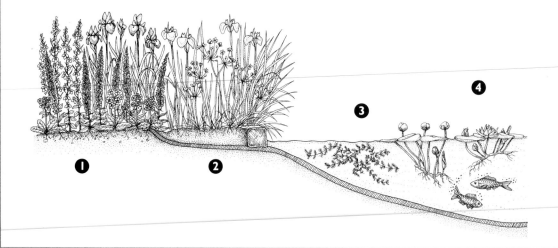

PLANTING AN ISLAND BED

These two cross-sections through island beds illustrate how the taller plants are placed in the centre and the shortest around the outside.

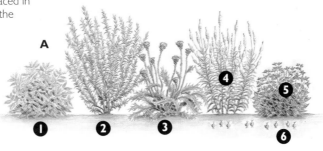

A Late summer on a dry soil. *Papaver orientale* 'Perry's White' has finished flowering, but the gap it leaves has been filled by *Linaria purpurea* 'Canon Went'. Crocuses flower in spring beneath the still-dormant origanum.

B Late summer on an average soil. The felicia on the left is a temporary half-hardy plant for the summer only; crocuses will flower on its site in the spring. The cosmos is a half-hardy annual; daffodils will flower in its position in spring.

C Early summer on a slightly moist soil. This cross-section illustrates an island bed in which the plants are not graded by height. Instead, it consists of a low drift of perennials. The *Geranium endressii* will flower on and off throughout the summer; the snowdrops flower in late winter around the still-dormant *Polemonium caeruleum*.

A
1 *Salvia officinalis* 'Purpurascens'
2 *Rosmarinus officinalis*
3 *Papaver orientale* 'Perry's White'
4 *Linaria purpurea* 'Canon Went'
5 *Origanum laevigatum* 'Herrenhausen'
6 Crocus bulbs

B
1 *Felicia bergeriana*
2 *Spiraea japonica* 'Little Princess'
3 *Miscanthus sinensis* 'Silberfeder'
4 *Cosmos bipinnatus* 'King George'
5 *Aster amellus* 'King George'
6 Crocus bulbs
7 Narcissus bulbs

C
1 *Geranium endressii*
2 *Filipendula ulmaria*
3 *Lychnis coronaria*
4 *Geranium* 'Spinners'
5 *Geranium endressii*
6 *Polemonium caeruleum*
7 Snowdrop (*Galanthus*) bulbs

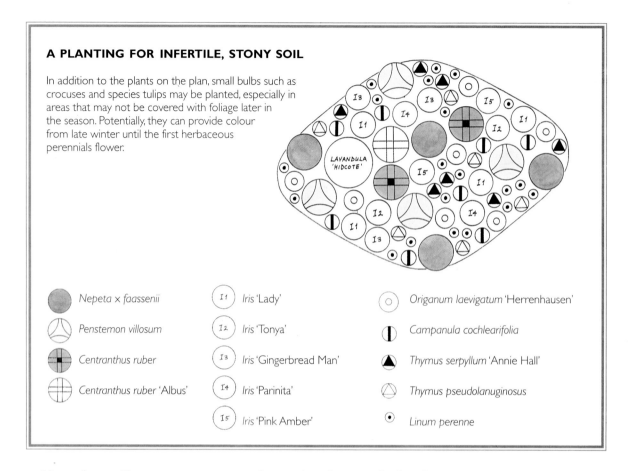

A PLANTING FOR INFERTILE, STONY SOIL

In addition to the plants on the plan, small bulbs such as crocuses and species tulips may be planted, especially in areas that may not be covered with foliage later in the season. Potentially, they can provide colour from late winter until the first herbaceous perennials flower.

Nepeta × faassenii	I1 — Iris 'Lady'	⊙ — Origanum laevigatum 'Herrenhausen'
Penstemon villosum	I2 — Iris 'Tonya'	Campanula cochleariifolia
Centranthus ruber	I3 — Iris 'Gingerbread Man'	Thymus serpyllum 'Annie Hall'
Centranthus ruber 'Albus'	I4 — Iris 'Parinita'	Thymus pseudolanuginosus
	I5 — Iris 'Pink Amber'	Linum perenne

Most of us will not want to surround a pool completely with vegetation; at least one side can be kept open to lawn or paving, with room for sitting by the pool and watching for pondlife. This open side should face the sun, so that the water receives good light. Full sun all day is not good for fish and other pond creatures, so shade at one end, or the shade of large-leaved plants, is beneficial.

ISLAND BEDS

Island beds free perennials and shrubs from the need for a backdrop of fence, hedge or wall. They are a useful way of breaking up wide expanses of lawn or, on a smaller scale, paving or gravel. To be successful, they need to be in proportion to the size of the area; beds that are too large overwhelm the surrounding space, while conversely those that are too small are themselves overwhelmed. This applies not only to the size of the bed but also to the plants in it – all too frequently a nice little shrub from the garden centre turns into a monster that occupies the entire bed and towers over its surroundings.

Island beds are a good way in which to display plants, especially lower growing ones, as you can walk all around them. This arrangement is also quite demanding of your planting skills, as more is on display than with a conventional border. There is no space, for instance, in which to hide the bare stems of leggy shrubs.

There are two approaches to island beds. The first is to mix taller shrubs with shorter ones and perennials to create a planting carefully graded by height, with the tallest in the middle and the shortest on the outside. This is a useful approach if you need some height to use the bed for screening or to break up an area visually. Such a planting can be combined with a small tree, but choose one with an erect habit of growth or it will shade out the rest of the bed. Another way of adding height is to incorporate a climber on a free-standing support.

If a tall island bed does not seem appropriate, a lower planting using perennials and low-growing shrubs is possible. Taller perennials and grasses can

A carefully chosen selection of strong-growing perennials, including pink Persicaria bistorta, *will reduce maintenance requirements dramatically.*

be used to create seasonal height, but will be cut down in winter. Plants can either be grouped so as to create eye-catching blocks of colour, or blended more naturalistically. Extending the concept of blended perennials in an island bed leads us 'beyond the border'.

BEYOND THE BORDER

Traditionally borders have been one-sided affairs, hugging a backdrop such as a wall or fence. Island beds at least liberated planting from being largely two dimensional, but modern European garden design is becoming more radical still, developing a planting style that involves creating wide drifts of colour using perennials and grasses, a bit like a wildflower meadow. This style undoubtedly looks best when carried out on a large scale, but I have seen many smaller gardens where it also works well. The great advantage of this style for the keen gardener is that it gives extra scope for growing more herbaceous plants and for giving them more space than in a conventional border. When an appropriate choice of plants is made, it is also easier to have a long season of interest and to reduce the maintenance that is necessary.

The key to the new style is to choose a selection of plants that look good together, and then scatter them in drifts across the planting area. The idea is to achieve rhythm through repetition, rather than planting one or two of everything, which just ends up looking messy. One way of doing this is to compose a planting made up of several groups of varieties that all flower at the same time and look attractive together, so that as the year progresses one group replaces another in succession. Early in the year the non-flowering groups are merely low clumps of green; later on those that have finished flowering are largely hidden by the group that is currently putting on its show.

Another important aspect of the new style is the way in which plants are grouped. Certain plants are by nature bold and imposing, miscanthus grasses for example, and with relatively wide spacing will

PLANTS FOR GROWING IN WALLS

For shady walls	For sunny walls	For very sunny, dry walls
Arenaria	*Alyssum saxatile*	*Cheiranthus* varieties
Asplenium and *Ceterach* species (ferns)	*Armeria* species	*Dianthus deltoides* and other small,
Haberlea rhodopensis	*Erinus alpinus*	cushion-forming dianthus
Ramonda myconi	*Erysimum alpinum*	*Helianthemum serpyllifolium*
	Gypsophila repens	*Lewisia cotyledon* hybrids
	Linaria alpina	*Phlox subulata*
	Saponaria ocymoides	
	Saxifraga species	
	Sedum species	
	Sempervivum species	

---

dominate a planting. Others, such as foxgloves (*Digitalis* species), need to be placed in loose groups or clumps to have much impact. Still others, generally the low-growing species, look best when grown as a continuous low carpet, either on their own or blended with other ground-hugging varieties.

PLANTING IN TUNE WITH NATURE

A vital part of the new movement in perennial planting is the stress put on choosing the right plants for a given environment. This will reduce the need for maintenance, as the plants will form a relatively stable community. For example, a fertile, moist soil would be planted up with robust perennials such as purple loosestrife (*Lythrum salicaria*) and geraniums, and their strong growth will make it difficult for weeds to compete. A poor, stony soil on the other hand is not an attractive environment for either weeds or robust garden plants, but it is ideal for species adapted to stressful situations, such as bearded irises, valerian (*Centranthus ruber*) and nepetas.

For the gardener who is interested in low maintenance and is quite open-minded about what to grow, this is an ideal approach, but for those with more time and a list of specific plants that they would like in the garden, it will be unsatisfactory. Such gardeners can certainly employ drift plantings, but they will have a greater task either in removing weeds from among the non-competitive plants or in soil modification to suit the kinds of plant they want to grow.

ROCK GARDENS AND RAISED BEDS

Rockeries are not my favourite garden feature. Usually they look awful, and just like what they are: piles of rock plonked where you would not expect a pile of rock. A well-made rock garden, however, is a delight, but it is one of the most difficult things to achieve. The key to success is to make it look as natural as possible, and good planting is part of the answer – too often a rock garden is planted with a couple of dwarf conifers, some heathers and aubrieta, and that is it. Yet the potential is enormous, because there are so many plants that thrive in the well-drained conditions that a well-constructed rock garden provides.

A good rockery should have plenty of variety. Its slopes can provide many different microclimates: a sunny side where dwarf thymes, oreganos and wild tulips can soak up the sun, a shady side for mossy saxifrages and ferns, and a partly shaded side for many other alpines.

Because of their small size, alpines cannot be combined easily with other garden plants and, by themselves, they make little impact on the garden as a whole. This may be one reason why a rockery so rarely looks appropriate in a garden. Raised beds offer an alternative method of growing alpines, as

*Valerian, thrift (*Armeria*) and a campanula spill out of a retaining wall, creating a splash of midsummer colour.*

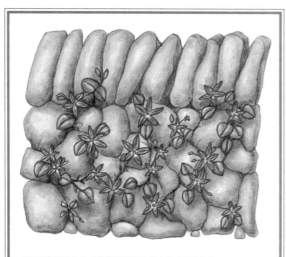

GROWING ALPINES IN A WALL

Some campanulas, especially *Campanula poscharskyana* (as here) and *C. portenschlagiana*, will penetrate the tiniest crack and throw out flowering stems over a wide area.

bricks or stones are removed here and there, new walls too can offer planting places. One possible way of getting plants to grow in holes that are too narrow to take them, is to mix seed of appropriate species into balls of earth and stuff the balls into the cracks.

PLANTING VERTICALLY

A vertical dimension may be present in a garden in the form of existing walls, or it can be added by means of various structures. The pergola, that rather Edwardian garden feature where climbers (mostly roses) are grown over a path, is a somewhat grandiose example. Archways have become popular of late, and they are rather more appropriate for the smaller garden. Then there are the clematis-draped obelisks that started to sprout in fashionable gardens not so long ago. All these devices enable climbing plants to be grown independently of walls and fences, and they play an important part in many successful gardens.

Most climbers have a character that fits best with romantic, old-fashioned gardens and those with pastel colour schemes. Walls with tumbling honeysuckles and roses are the vital backdrop to a cottage-style garden, and an archway covered with climbers makes an appropriate exit and entry from one part of the garden to another. Obelisks or other free-standing plant supports are a very useful way of introducing climbers into borders, where their flowers or foliage can play an integral part in the planting scheme, and a can take on more central role than perhaps they would simply planted on a wall or fence.

Some climbers look magnificent growing on houses; indeed, we automatically associate *Clematis montana* with country cottages and wisteria with the Georgian style of architecture. Roses and honeysuckle are great favourites, and nothing beats their fragrance wafting in through an open window on a sunny day. In my opinion, the possibilities for using climbers on houses are not generally explored enough. Growing several climbers together is particularly effective: an early honeysuckle can be combined with a late-flowering clematis, for example, creating a longer season of flower colour.

A freer use of climbers is to grow them as nature intended, scrambling over other plants. Roses

well as other plants that like good drainage, and are much easier to fit visually into the garden. They can be constructed so that the alpines grow out of the walls as well as in the bed in the top, thus allowing the hard surface of the stone to be softened. They are also a good means of creating divisions in a garden and, since they are raised, will add elevation.

Alpines can be grown so that they present a landscape in miniature – the very first rockeries had toy mountain goats on them!– and in a tiny garden this can be a very creative way of increasing the psychological and visual space. In any garden these plants, and their accompanying raised bed or rockery, will look a lot better if thought is given to providing some sort of appropriate context. A small conifer – a spruce, pine or juniper, such as one might find on a mountainside – makes an appropriate backdrop.

GROWING IN WALLS

One of the most adventurous ways of growing alpines is in walls. Old walls with crumbling mortar and plenty of holes are ideal in this context, and can provide homes for a large number of plants. Newer walls present a less hospitable environment, but if

Left: Climbers can be used to wonderfully romantic effect on gateposts. This is Vitis coignetiae *in autumn.*

Above: Pyracantha is ideal for training neatly against walls, making a fiery spectacle with its winter berries.

growing up old apple trees in cottage gardens can be seen fairly frequently, but there is no reason why we should not be more adventurous. I have seen summer-flowering clematis used over spring-flowering shrubs, and even trailing over winter-flowering heathers. Such situations demand varieties that can be cut back over the winter to allow the earlier-flowering plant beneath to perform unencumbered.

PLANTING TO DIRECT THE VIEW

When we look at a garden, our eyes do not sweep uniformly over it. We are attracted by particular things, so that our attention is focused on some parts of the scene at the expense of others. By clever manipulation of the planting and the use of features such as archways, pergolas and garden ornaments, it is possible to control the viewer's gaze. Most fundamentally, it is important to be able to hide eyesores – the garage, a neighbour's extension or the gasworks over the road.

Eyesores can generally be hidden by planting a screen in front of them or, in the case of buildings on your own land, with climbers. Usually it is not important that the plants you use are especially beautiful in their own right, but rather that they are fast growing. Since an eyesore is an eyesore, whether it is winter or summer, evergreens are preferable, although in the case of climbers the choice is unfortuantely very limited. The rapid-growing leyland cypress (x *Cupressocyparis leylandii*) might seem an attractive option for screening, but given that it sucks moisture and nutrients out of the soil and casts a dour shade, it can become a problem in its own right. The ideal screening tree is narrow in shape and light in aspect; tree of heaven (*Ailanthus altissima*) is a good deciduous option, *Prunus avium* – an attractive large cherry – another, and willows a third. Good evergreens that do not grow too wide are eucalyptus and (in warm climates) acacias.

As well as hiding unwanted features, it is good to be able to enhance desirable ones and to direct the gaze to other parts of the garden, without making it all visible at once. Arches and gateways hung with climbers not only draw the eye, they also focus it on what can be seen through them. A particularly interesting specimen or planting can also draw the eye to it, and thence onward to something not so immediately visible: a distant view, perhaps, or another part of the garden. However, the effect can be spoilt if the 'eyecatcher' is so effective that it leaps forward, shortening the perspective in the garden. A classic example of this is the magenta azalea that is planted on the far side of the garden but that is so bright that it almost yells for attention, to the detriment of everything else.

CONTAINERS

Containers are ideal for temporary plantings to liven up the area around the house or other high-profile areas, but they are also valuable for more permanent schemes where soil is limited, such as in backyards and on roof gardens and balconies. In some countries they are virtually *de rigeur* – the windowboxes that drip scarlet pelargoniums in Austria and Switzerland, for example. Elsewhere, containers are growing in popularity and

inventiveness in planting them is ever increasing.

Whether a container is for permanent or seasonal planting, it is important that the plants are in keeping with it, especially if the container is rather fine. Proportion is very important: plants that are tall or top-heavy will make the whole

composition look unbalanced (they may make it physically unstable as well), but if they are too low, the container will dominate completely. These rules can be relaxed a bit when several containers are put together, as a very tall plant can be put at the back and balanced visually by others.

Drifts of herbaceous plants, including creamy Artemisia lactiflora, *border a patch which leads the eye on into the rest of the garden.*

PLANTING IN CONTAINERS

A plant does not have the resources in a container that it does in the ground, and consequently both watering and feeding need to be regular. Hi-tech solutions have made life somewhat easier, with water-holding gels and slow-release, long-life fertilizers now widely available.

Holes in the bottom of containers are an absolute must to allow excess water to drain away, otherwise root rot will set in rapidly. Compost in a container heats up and cools down more rapidly than soil in a border. During the winter, bubble plastic or another insulating material can be wrapped around the pots to help prevent freezing, or the pots can be brought indoors when deep frost threatens.

A blend of colour can be very pleasing, and the most successful plantings often involve one flower that echoes the colour of the container. It is not a good idea to cram very ornate pots with a number of contrasting plants or plants with small and intricate foliage – a simple, bold statement made by one or two large-leaved plants will always be much more appropriate.

SEASONAL PLANTINGS

The vast majority of container plantings are for the summer season. Colourful exuberance is achieved with long-flowering pelargoniums, lobelias, petunias and other bedding plants, but increasingly gardeners are experimenting with other more subtle but equally long-lasting plant combinations, using herbs, plants with coloured foliage, grasses and even vegetables in their containers.

Plants for seasonal colour need to be quick growing in order to show results, but not so

Above: An agave, pelargoniums, marguerites and succulent echeverias form an attractive pastel composition for a summer patio.

vigorous that they will behave like cuckoos in the nest and starve the other plants. Ideally, they should not be moisture-lovers; it is a hot, and often dry, life in a pot all summer. Containers usually look better if they are planted with a limited number of plants in a tight colour scheme, than if a thousand and one varieties are stuffed in together.

While summer is the main time of year for container plants, spring schemes are an excellent way of bringing the season a little nearer to the house, which is especially valuable for those with limited garden space or even none at all. Bulbs, polyanthus and other spring flowers make excellent container plants, and they can all be planted out in the garden when they have finished flowering. If this is not possible, keep them in a light but cool place for the summer. Winter containers can be surprisingly colourful if planted with pansies, winter heathers, dwarf hebes and grasses with attractive winter leaves.

PERMANENT PLANTINGS

Permanently planted containers are the answer if you have no garden. It is vital that the plants chosen are not so vigorous that they will outgrow their container in one season and then starve. Since they are permanent, they will need to be attractive for as much of the year as possible. It is not surprising that evergreens, especially those with coloured or variegated foliage, are so popular for this purpose. In Mediterranean countries there is also a great tradition of growing evergreen topiary in containers, often in imaginative and extravagant shapes. Herbs are also successful and attractive in pots, and very practical.

The best permanent plants for containers are those that are relatively slow growing, which eliminates most herbaceous perennials. Slow- and low-growing shrubs are generally the most successful, particularly if they are shallow rooted, like camellias and rhododendrons.

BEDDING-OUT CONTAINER PLANTS

Very popular in Victorian times, and now due for a revival, is the practice of planting out tender plants in pots for the summer, immersing them in the soil to allow them to merge with the surrounding plants. In times gone by, whole borders would be filled with palms, bananas and other exotica surrounded by bedding, whereas today's practitioners like to combine their plants with hardy species.

Over the summer there is a great tendency for the roots of the plants to run through the holes in the pot and into the soil of the border, which can result in considerable damage to the plants when they are taken up in the autumn. This can be avoided to some extent by ensuring that they are potted on before planting out, or by taking them out of their pots for the summer and repotting on lifting in the autumn.

This technique can be extended by using pots full of greenhouse- or conservatory-raised flowering plants as temporary gap fillers in summer borders, sometimes for only a few weeks – an especially useful trick early in the season. It is amazing how many people are fooled by this ploy, thinking that the plants are actually growing in the ground.

'Hot' colours make the most of summer. Here, pots of variegated abutilon, lantana and soft orange Mimulus aurantiacus *share paving space.*

PLANTING
PLANS

A PLANTING FOR SPRING

FLOWERS ARE PERHAPS more important in spring than at any other time of year, for after the winter is when we appreciate them most, particularly when they are close to the house. This site is on the side of the house, where it receives light for half the day or less and there is little space for planting.

The narrow beds contain a selection of spring-flowering, shade-tolerant perennials, such as lily-of-the-valley (*Convallaria majalis*), and bulbs,

plus tall plants like a bamboo and an early-flowering mahonia, to make the best use of the limited space. A small bed has been made in the middle of the paved area for spring-flowering shrubs and perennials, and pots of daffodils have been brought in for extra colour.

Shade-tolerant climbers are also included, all self-clinging varieties apart from the honeysuckle (*Lonicera japonica* 'Halliana') on the left, which clambers over a trellis concealing an oil tank.

MAINTENANCE – *Low*

Nearly all these plants require little maintenance, an annual clear-up of dead stems and leaves being all that is needed. The daffodils in pots are best planted out in the open ground when they have finished, and new bulbs bought for the following year's display. The camellia in a tub should be fed regularly throughout the growing season, and never allowed to dry out. During the winter, the container must be surrounded with bubble plastic to prevent the roots from freezing.

SITE AND SEASON

This planting requires sun for only a few hours a day. Any reasonably fertile and well-drained soil is suitable – the soil around buildings is often full of rubble, which may mean that annual manuring and feeding is necessary in order to provide good growing conditions.

The main flowering is in mid-spring. Although there will be few flowers for the rest of the year, the foliage of all these plants is attractive in its own right. Annuals and half-hardy plants in containers could be brought in for the summer and stood in the lighter areas.

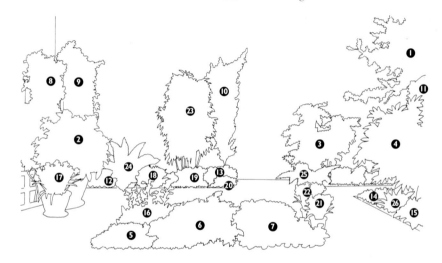

Trees
1 *Prunus* 'Pandora'

Shrubs
2 *Camellia* 'Anticipation'
3 *Mahonia* × *media* 'Charity'
4 *Fatsia japonica*
5 *Daphne* × *burkwoodii*
6 *Mahonia aquifolium*
7 *Rhododendron williamsianum*

Climbers
8 *Lonicera japonica* 'Halliana'
9 *Parthenocissus henryana*
10 *Hedera helix* 'Sagittifolia Variegata'

11 *Hedera canariensis* 'Variegata'

Perennials
12 *Brunnera macrophylla* 'Dawson's White'
13 *Pulmonaria saccharata* 'Leopard'
14 *Epimedium* × *rubrum*
15 *Convallaria majalis*
16 *Symphytum* × *uplandicum* 'Variegatum'

Bulbs
17 *Narcissus* 'Mount Hood'
18 *Narcissus* 'Portrush'
19 *Hyacinthoides hispanica*

20 *Cyclamen repandum*
21 *Narcissus* 'Actaea'
22 *Narcissus* 'Golden Harvest'

Grasses
23 *Phyllostachys nigra*

Ferns
24 *Polystichum munitum*
25 *Polystichum setiferum* 'Divisilobum Densum'
26 *Asplenium scolopendrium*

A SHOWY SUMMER PLANTING

I OFTEN HEAR GARDENERS complaining about mid- to late summer as being a boring time in the garden. Here is just one of many possible plantings for this season. In fact, it is a potentially exciting time of year as there are lots of hardy perennials in flower, and plenty of more exotic half-hardy plants that are just getting into

their stride; annuals and bedding plants are likewise coming to maturity.

This planting scheme is based on pinks and blues. It includes a lot of strong foliage shapes and some interesting and rather stylishly shaped flowers. The overall effect is rather exotic, and ideal for enhancing your enjoyment of hot weather.

MAINTENANCE – *Medium*

While the core of the varieties here are hardy, requiring only an annual clearing away of dead stems, some of the planting's panache comes from half-hardy species that either need lifting or protecting for the winter. Among the hardies, *Dahlia merckii* might suffer in cold regions and should be protected with straw or bubble plastic. The half-hardies will need to be stored in a frost-free greenhouse for the winter in most areas. the cannas and *Salvia patens* die down to tubers, making for easy storage. Among the annuals, the nemophila is a hardy one which can be sown outside in spring. The others will need to be raised from seed in a greenhouse and planted out after the last frost.

SITE AND SEASON

Any reasonably fertile soil is suitable, but preferably one that does not dry out too quickly. This planting needs a warm position to do well, and certainly somewhere that receives sun for most of the day.

The flowering season is mid- to late summer.

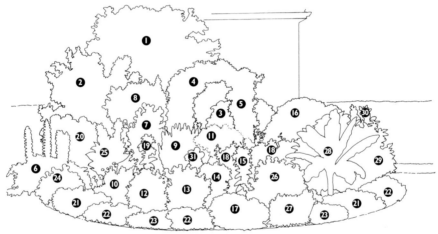

Trees

1 *Hoheria lyallii*

Shrubs

2 *Hibiscus syriacus* 'Woodbridge'
3 *Hydrangea quercifolia*

Climbers

4 *Passiflora caerulea*
5 *Clematis* 'Etoile Violette'

Perennials

6 *Acanthus spinosus*
7 *Echinops* 'Nivalis'
8 *Macleaya microcarpa* 'Kelway's Coral Plume'
9 *Lythrum salicaria*
10 *Dahlia merckii*
11 *Artemisia lactiflora*
12 *Penstemon* 'Sour Grapes'
13 *Penstemon* 'Garnet'
14 *Penstemon* 'Blackbird'
15 *Verbena patagonica*
16 *Romneya coulteri*
17 *Limonium latifolium*

Bulbs

18 *Lilium* 'Journey's End'
19 *Lilium* 'Sterling Silver'

Annuals/biennials

20 *Cleome hassleriana*
21 *Brachyscombe iberidifolia*
22 *Impatiens* hybrids
23 *Nemophila menziesii*

Half-hardy

24 *Pelargonium quercifolium*
25 *Canna* 'Orchid'
26 *Salvia involucrata* 'Bethellii'
27 *Salvia patens*
28 *Musa basjoo*
29 *Datura arborea*
30 *Canna* 'Wyoming'
31 *Dahlia* 'White Klankstad'

A PLANTING FOR AUTUMN

AUTUMN HAS TREMENDOUS potential, not just for the reds and yellows of trees and the wide range of colours that berries offer. but also for the number of flowers that are at their best at this time. It is difficult to fit many trees into a small garden. but there a several shrubs that are just as colourful, together with a number of climbers. The most valuable are those, like the amelanchier, sorbus and euonymus used here. which combine attractive fruit with good leaf colour.

The larger autumn flowers are nearly all members of the daisy family. The violet, purple and blue shades come from the asters, the yellow from *Solidago* 'Crown of Rays'. The best way to grow these plants is to mix them in with spring- and summer-flowering shrubs and perennials, so that they are not particularly noticeable until they flower. There are certain bulbs that bloom now: cyclamen will flourish in difficult places, such as deep shade in dry soil under trees, while colchicums make bold splashes of pink in borders or rough grass. Ornamental grasses are another special autumn feature, with the advantage that they will carry on looking good until well into the winter. Low winter light and hoar frost show them off to their best.

MAINTENANCE – Low to Medium

Most of these plants require little care and attention. The herbaceous flowering varieties can be cut down at any time from early to late winter, but the grasses are sufficiently ornamental to make them worth keeping until later on. Many of these grasses and late-flowering plants produce seed that helps feed bird populations through the winter, which is another reason to delay cutting back. The late-flowering members of the daisy family appreciate a good, fertile soil, so a mulch of well-rotted manure or garden compost is a good idea in spring, especially on poorer soils. The asters here require little maintenance, but will benefit from dividing and replanting every few years.

SITE AND SEASON

Any reasonably fertile, well-drained soil is suitable for this scheme. Choose a site that receives sun for most of the day.

The flowering season is from late summer to early winter, although autumn colour and flowers do depend a lot on the weather. Late flowering perennials are easy to combine with earlier flowering species and bulbs. Since they tend to look a bit untidy after flowering, put them behind the late flowering plants and grasses which, as they grow neatly through the summer, will help to hide them.

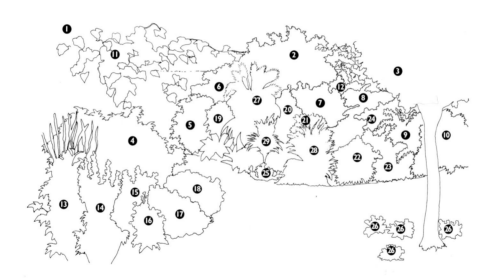

Trees
1 *Quercus coccinea* 'Splendens'
2 *Amelanchier canadensis*
3 *Malus tschonoskii*

Shrubs
4 *Acer palmatum* 'Osakazuki'
5 *Euonymus europaeus* 'Red Cascade'
6 *Sorbus vilmorinii*
7 *Pyracantha* 'Orange Glow'
8 *Cotoneaster horizontalis*

9 *Fuchsia magellanica* 'Riccartonii'
10 *Acer palmatum* var. *dissectum*

Climbers
11 *Vitis coignetiae*
12 *Parthenocissus quinquefolia*

Perennials
13 *Cimicifuga racemosa*
14 *Aconitum carmichaelii*
15 *Eupatorium rugosum*

16 *Serratula tinctoria*
17 *Aster × frikartii* 'Mönch'
18 *Aster ericoides* 'Blue Star'
19 *Vernonia crinita*
20 *Leucanthemum serotinum*
21 *Aster cordifolius* 'Little Carlow'
22 *Aster amellus* 'King George'
23 *Solidago* 'Crown of Rays'
24 *Aster* 'Climax'

Bulbs
25 *Colchicum agrippinum*
26 *Cyclamen hederifolium*

Grasses
27 *Miscanthus sinensis* 'Silberfeder'
28 *Panicum virgatum*
29 *Molinia caerulea* 'Variegata'

A TACTILE AND FRAGRANT GARDEN

THIS PLANTING IS DESIGNED primarily with the partially sighted in mind, but it should serve to remind all of us of the importance of stimulating senses other than sight in the garden.

There is a considerable variety of plants with scented flowers for a wide range of seasons, together with several species that have aromatic foliage, such as the scented-leaved pelargoniums and lemon verbena (*Aloysia triphylla*). It is quite a good idea to place such plants around a seating area; some are potent enough to release their scent on being brushed against, and all can be a stimulus to conversation.

Touch is an underrated element in the garden: leaf shapes and textures vary enormously, from the smoothness of *Magnolia grandiflora* 'Exmouth' to the roughness of witch hazel (*Hamamelis* x *intermedia* 'Pallida'). Many plants have tactile seedheads, too, such as honesty (*Lunaria annua*) and the quaking grass (*Briza maxima*), and flowers, like bleeding heart (*Dicentra spectabilis*).

MAINTENANCE – *Medium*

Most of the plants here are shrubs or perennials which require little attention. The annuals and biennials, though, will need to be sown every year, although honesty usually manages to do this for itself.

The plants in containers, and the pelargoniums, will have to be kept in the house or in a greenhouse over the winter, ideally above freezing point, or above -4°C (25°F) if they are kept dry.

SITE AND SEASON

Any reasonably fertile, well-drained soil is suitable for this garden. The wall facing the patio also faces the sun, with the plants immediately against it appreciating good summer heat. Those on the far left are the most shade tolerant.

The main flowering is in early summer.

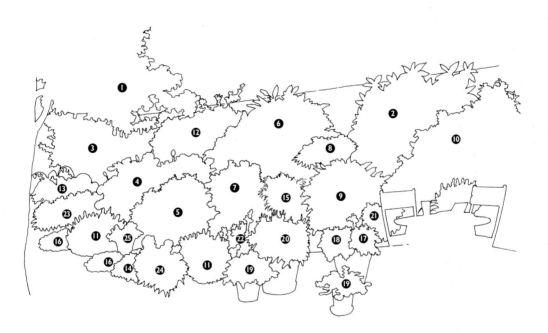

Trees
1 *Populus* × *candicans*
2 *Magnolia grandiflora* 'Exmouth'

Shrubs
3 *Hamamelis* × *intermedia* 'Pallida'
4 *Rosa* 'Madame Isaac Pereire'
5 *Choisya ternata*
6 *Cytisus battandieri*
7 *Viburnum* × *carlcephalum*
8 *Euphorbia mellifera*
9 *Syringa* × *persica*

10 *Philadelphus* 'Belle Etoile'
11 *Lavandula stoechas* 'Pedunculata'

Climbers
12 *Lonicera caprifolium*

Perennials
13 *Dicentra spectabilis*
14 *Mentha suaveolens* 'Variegata'
15 *Foeniculum vulgare*
16 *Thymus* × *citriodorus* 'Aureus'

Half-hardy
17 *Pelargonium* 'Chocolate Peppermint'
18 *Pelargonium odoratissimum*
19 *Pelargonium* 'Royal Oak'
20 *Aloysia citriodora*

Annuals/biennials
21 *Matthiola* 'Giant Imperial'
22 *Lathyrus odoratus* 'Knee Hi'
23 *Lunaria annua*
24 *Dianthus barbatus* Monarch Series
25 *Briza maxima*

A HERB GARDEN

IT IS CONVENIENT for the cook to have herbs growing together in one place, and preferably near to the kitchen door. Most herbs are reasonably attractive plants, so a herb garden can be quite ornamental in its own right. It can be further enhanced by interspersing the herbs with some purely decorative cottage-garden flowers and old-fashioned roses. Access to the herbs needs to be easy, so paths are always an important feature of herb gardens.

The planting of low box hedges is a fashionable part of making a herb garden, but is inadvisable in small spaces because of the tendency of the questing box roots to take moisture and nutrients away from the herbs. A good alternative to box is dwarf lavender.

MAINTENANCE – *Medium to high*

Most herbs are perennial, needing only an autumn cut back if they become untidy. Others are either annual (basil) or biennial (parsley) and so will need to be sown afresh from seed every year.

Since herb plants are being constantly cropped, it will be necessary to feed the soil, either with an annual application of manure in the autumn or fertilizer in spring.

Some herbs – mints are especially notorious – have very invasive roots that can lead to them becoming weeds. One way of constricting the roots is to plant them in a half-barrel with the bottom knocked out, which is buried in the soil to a depth of about 30cm (12in).

SITE AND SEASON

This herb garden requires sun for most of the day. Any reasonably fertile and well-drained soil would be suitable.

Most of the herbs flower in midsummer. Bulbs and cottage-garden annuals can be added for earlier and later colour.

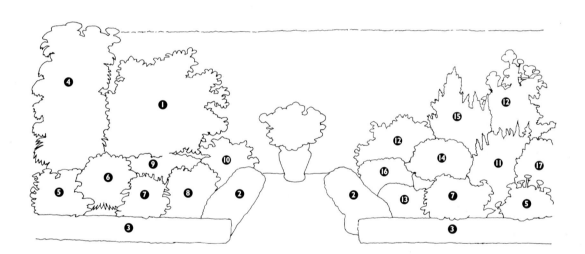

Shrubs

1 *Rosa* 'Ispahan'
2 *Lavandula angustifolia* 'Munstead'
3 *Buxus sempervirens* 'Suffruticosa'

Herbs

4 Purple fennel (*Foeniculum vulgare* 'Purpureum')
5 English marigold (*Calendula officinalis*)

6 Chives (*Allium schoenoprasum*)
7 Sweet basil (*Ocimum basilicum*)
8 Sweet marjorum (*Origanum majorana*)
9 Parsley 'Champion Moss Curled' (*Petroselinum crispum*)
10 Chervil (*Anthriscus cerefolium*)
11 Sage (*Salvia officinalis*)

12 Lovage (*Levisticum officinale*)
13 Thyme (*Thymus vulgaris*)
14 Peppermint (*Mentha* × *piperita*)
15 Rosemary (*Rosmarinus officinalis*)
16 Purple sage (*Salvia officinalis* 'Purpurascens')
17 Summer savory (*Satureia hortensis*)

A ROSE GARDEN

ROSE GARDENS are a traditional feature of parks and gardens, yet they are often gaunt and bare for much of the year and feature only modern hybrids with scentless flowers in garish pinks and oranges.

This rose garden is different. It concentrates on the old-fashioned varieties, with flowers mostly in subtle shades of pink, and nearly all have an excellent scent. Many of the older roses flower only once in the season, but the selection here will either flower continuously from early to late summer or will repeat flower in late summer after their main, early summer season.

Roses look so much better when grown in company with geraniums, artemisias and various other perennials. These not only complement the colours of the roses but also minimize weeding underneath them.

MAINTENANCE – *Medium*

Older rose varieties do not need the rigorous annual pruning that is customary for modern hybrids. In fact, if in doubt – leave alone! Pruning should really be left until the plants are becoming too big and untidy for their situation. Then it should be carried out in late winter, removing dead and unhealthy-looking stems, and any that are relatively thin and weak, crossing or overcrowded. The remaining strong stems should be cut back by one-third. Feeding and manuring need be carried out only on poor or sandy soils.

The perennials featured here need only be cut back in late autumn. However, for the first two or three years of the roses' lives the perennials should be be kept away from their bases, so that the roots can become established.

SITE AND SEASON

This garden requires a site in full sun. While deep and fertile soils are the best for roses, this selection has been chosen to do well on poorer soils than roses would normally thrive on. As much as possible should be done to enrich poor soils by mulching with well-rotted manure, or by using a combination of garden compost and feeding.

The garden will be at its peak in early summer, but most of the roses will flower off and on until early autumn, as will the pink geraniums. Bulbs can be added for spring interest.

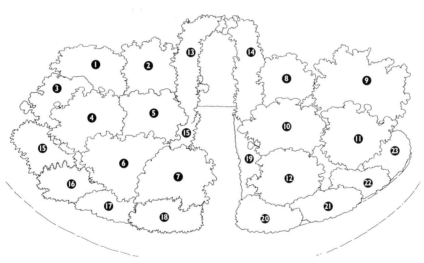

Roses

1 *Rosa rugosa* 'Alba'
2 'Gloire de Ducher'
3 'Comte de Chambord'
4 'Reine des Violettes'
5 'Charles Lefèbvre'
6 'La Reine Victoria'
7 'Louise Odier'
8 'Ferdinand Pichard'
9 'Roseraie de l'Haÿ'
10 'Jacques Cartier'
11 'Baroness Rothschild'
12 'Rose de Rescht'

Climbing Roses

13 'Souvenir de Docteur Jamain'
14 'Swan Lake'

Perennials

15 *Pulmonaria saccharata*
16 *Artemisia canescens*
17 *Geranium* × *oxonianum* 'Wargrave Pink'
18 *Artemisia ludoviciana*

19 *Galium odoratum*
20 *Geranium himalayense*
21 *Geranium* × *oxonianum* 'Winscombe'
22 *Geranium endressii*
23 *Geranium versicolor*

A WHITE BORDER

VITA SACKVILLE-WEST certainly started a fashion with her white garden at Sissinghurst. The great thing about white is its coolness, and the feeling of calm repose that it generates. As for choosing the plants, the task is relatively easy as so many coloured species have a white form (*alba* in Latin), although you will soon find that many so-called 'white' flowers (like 'white' walls) are really cream or very pale something else. I have restricted the selection here largely to pure whites, and the variegated and grey-leaved plants that combine so well with them.

Given the choice of plants, it is possible to create white gardens in a variety of different soils and situations, so this is a very flexible colour scheme. There should be no problems, either, in finding plants to keep the scheme going until autumn.

MAINTENANCE – Medium to low

The majority of these are easy and vigorous plants, so little maintenance is required, except for the usual autumn clear-up and perhaps a mulching with well-rotted manure or garden compost. With the exception of the shrub roses, which must be pruned in late winter, the shrubs should be pruned after flowering if they need it.

SITE AND SEASON

Any reasonably fertile soil and a site that receives sun for most of the day will be suitable.

The main flowering season is midsummer, although there are so many white flowers available that there is no problem extending the season. Bulbs, such as snowdrops and ivory-white daffodils, are especially easy to interplant between the shrubs and perennials. White asters and other daisy relatives can be planted for autumn.

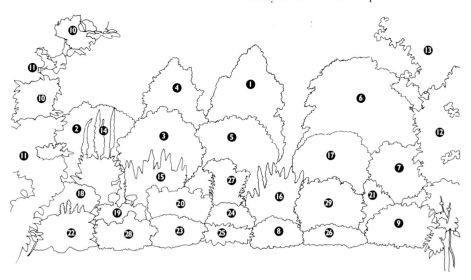

Trees
1 *Eucryphia* × *nymansensis* 'Nymansay'

Shrubs
2 *Rubus* 'Benenden'
3 *Rosa* 'Boule de Neige'
4 *Abutilon vitifolium* var. *album*
5 *Choisya ternata*
6 *Cornus alternifolia* 'Variegata'
7 *Rosa* 'Iceberg'
8 *Hebe pinguifolia* 'Pagei'
9 *Cistus corbariensis*

Climbers
10 *Solanum jasminoides* 'Album'

11 *Rosa* 'Long John Silver'
12 *Jasminum officinale*
13 *Clematis* 'Alba Luxurians'

Perennials
14 *Digitalis purpurea* f. *albiflorum*
15 *Epilobium angustifolium* var. *album*
16 *Dictamnus albus*
17 *Crambe cordifolia*
18 *Achillea ptarmica* 'The Pearl'
19 *Papaver orientale* 'Perry's White'
20 *Anaphalis margaritacea*
21 *Libertia grandiflora*
22 *Hosta sieboldiana*

23 *Geranium clarkei* 'Kashmir White'
24 *Geranium renardii*
25 *Pulmonaria officinalis* 'Sissinghurst White'
26 *Lamium maculatum* 'White Nancy'

Bulbs
27 *Lilium* 'Sterling Silver'

Half-hardy
28 *Osteospermum* 'Whirligig'
29 *Argyranthemum frutescens*

A PASTEL BORDER

IDEAL FOR CLIMATES with grey skies, where every subtle nuance of tint and hue can be appreciated, and also for those gardeners new to border planning, it is almost impossible to go wrong with pastel combinations. There is a huge variety of plants with flowers in shades of blue, mauve and pink, and plenty too of the silver- and purple-leaved species that set them off so well. A limited number of pale yellow flowers can also be blended in; deep yellow and orange would destroy the effect of romantic softness. One or two scarlet flowers are possibly permissible, but dark crimson fits in better. Many of these flowers are fragrant, especially the roses. Old-fashioned and shrub roses are the most appropriate for this kind of planting, their flowers coming in a huge variety of shades of pink, setting the tone for the rest of the border.

Given the large number of plants that may be fitted into this colour scheme, there is no shortage of varieties that can carry it through the summer until early autumn.

MAINTENANCE – *Medium to low*

As it consists mainly of robust perennials and shrubs, this border requires little care. The roses are not the kind that need annual pruning, but if they begin to get untidy or too large they should be pruned in late winter. The other shrubs should be pruned after flowering. The lavatera is notorious for becoming very big very quickly, so make sure it is given plenty of space and be prepared to cut it back, preferably in late winter.

An annual tidy-up will be needed in autumn, and a mulch with well-rotted manure or garden compost will help maintain fertility, especially if the soil is at all poor. The roses and peony will certainly appreciate this

SITE AND SEASON

This scheme is suitable for any reasonably fertile soil that receives sun for most of the day.

The main period of flower is in early summer.

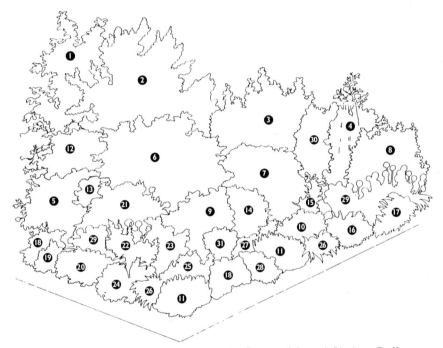

Trees
1 *Prunus* 'Spire'
2 *Cercis siliquastrum*

Shrubs
3 *Lavatera* 'Barnsley'
4 *Rosa* 'Reine Victoria'
5 *Rosa* 'Souvenir de la Malmaison'
6 *Ceanothus impressus*
7 *Syringa microphylla* 'Superba'
8 *Cotinus coggygria* 'Royal Purple'
9 *Cistus ladanifer*

10 *Rosa* 'The Fairy'
11 *Lavandula angustifolia* 'Munstead'

Climbers
12 *Clematis montana* 'Elizabeth'

Perennials
13 *Thalictrum aquilegifolium*
14 *Hesperis matronalis*
15 *Symphytum* × *uplandicum*
16 *Dicentra* 'Boothman's Variety'
17 *Polemonium foliosissimum*

18 *Geranium* 'Johnson's Blue'
19 *Lamium maculatum album*
20 *Geranium* × *oxonianum* 'Wargrave Pink'
21 *Paeonia lactiflora* 'Sarah Bernhardt'
22 *Campanula persicifolia*
23 *Anthemis tinctoria* 'E.C. Buxton'
24 *Alchemilla alpina*
25 *Campanula* 'Burghaltii'
26 *Ophiopogon planiscapus* 'Nigrescens'
27 *Artemisia ludoviciana*
28 *Dianthus* 'Doris'

Bulbs
29 *Allium aflatunense*

Annuals/biennials
30 *Lathyrus odoratus* 'Selana'

Half-hardy
31 *Argyranthemum* 'Mary Wootton'

A HOT BORDER

Reds and yellows are not colours for the fainthearted or those unsure of their skill at combining different shades. These are not relaxing colours, and they can be overpowering in a small garden. For those brave enough to try their hand, however, the results can glow magnificently.

Too much red can be quite oppressive, and too much bright yellow harsh and glaring. The trick is to mix them, so that they flicker together in a multiplicity of shades, and to be aware of the possibilities offered by dark purple and yellow foliage, and by good fresh greens that will complement the scarlet.

When selecting plants you will find that a lot of the best reds are half-hardy – many salvias, pelargoniums and cupheas (the cigar plant),for example – but they make up for this by being very long flowering, and flowering towards the end of the season, which many gardeners find a difficult time to make interesting. The exotic aspects of 'hot' planting should be played up, perhaps with some large foliage plants, like the castor oil plant, *Ricinus communis*. Such a planting is an exciting alternative to the traditional bedding that is often the mainstay of late summer. Hot-coloured flowers are not generally noted for their fragrance, but *Salvia rutilans* has wonderfully scented leaves.

MAINTENANCE – *Medium*

The dahlia, cuphea and chrysanthemum are definitely half-hardy and will need to be lifted and taken inside for the winter in most areas. The cuphea and chrysanthemum should be kept in a greenhouse or on a light windowsill, but the dahlias die back to convenient tubers. The salvia and erythrina are tender, but will survive the winter outside if the roots are well insulated. The annual perilla has to be started off indoors from seed, but the nasturtium (*Tropaeolum majus*) can be sown where it is to flower. The herbaceous plants will simply need their dead stems cut back in late autumn.

SITE AND SEASON

This border needs a sheltered corner which receives sun nearly all day, but with the right-hand side in sun for only half the day. Any reasonably fertile soil will be suitable.

The main flowering is in late summer, with many varieties looking good until well into the autumn. The main red and yellow season may be late summer, but there is not too much problem in extending it. Spring is easy, with all those yellow daffodils, tulips and polyanthus in almost any strong colour you want.

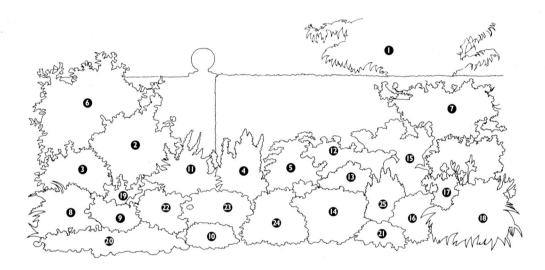

Trees

1 *Eucalyptus gunnii*

Shrubs

2 *Fremontodendron californicum*
3 *Euonymus japonicus* 'Aureopictus'
4 *Phygelius capensis coccineus*
5 *Berberis thunbergii* f. *atropurpurea*

Climbers

6 *Campsis* × *tagliabuana* 'Madame Galen'
7 *Tropaeolum speciosum*

Perennials

8 *Crocosmia* 'Lucifer'
9 *Oenothera fruticosa* 'Fireworks'
10 *Potentilla atrosanguinea*
11 *Erythrina crista-galli*
12 *Helenium* 'Wyndley'
13 *Monarda* 'Squaw'
14 *Coreopsis verticillata*
15 *Ligularia dentata* 'Desdemona'
16 *Rudbeckia fulgida* 'Goldsturm'
17 *Hemerocallis* 'Stafford'
18 *Hemerocallis* 'Golden Chimes'

Bulbs

19 *Lilium* 'Lady Bowes Lyon'

Annuals/biennials

20 *Tropaeolum majus*
21 *Perilla frutescens*

Half-hardy

22 *Dahlia* 'Bishop of Llandaff'
23 *Argyranthemum frutescens* 'Jamaica Primrose'
24 *Cuphea ignea*
25 *Salvia rutilans*

A FAR EASTERN LOOK

No one but the Japanese can make (or understand) a real Japanese garden, but we can attempt a version that suits us well enough. While most of the plants featured here are traditional in Japanese gardens, the key is to find plants that look Japanese in this kind of setting, even if they are not. *Alchemilla mollis* is one; its subtlety and elegance seem just right.

Bamboos, of course, are a must in setting the right mood, as are carefully placed stones and an overall emphasis on form and texture rather than colour. Nevertheless, colour does play a part, and can be surprisingly bright:

the year might start off with camellias and proceed to azaleas, which are among the most dazzling of all shrubs. However, the classic Japanese flowering plants are the well-known flowering cherries (*Prunus* species), and the less-often-grown *Iris ensata*.

Through its spareness and frugality, Japanese garden style is ideally suited to modern architecture. Ideally one would incorporate various props, such as lanterns and bamboo screens, into a planting such as this. They are, however, difficult to obtain and expensive. Good planting should be enough to create that distinctive oriental feel.

MAINTENANCE – *Low*

The emphasis here is on slow-growing foliage plants, which need little pruning and produce hardly any debris to clear away. Wisteria, however, takes a long time to get going and needs very careful pruning to encourage it to flower – for best results a pruning guide should be consulted.

SITE AND SEASON

Any reasonably fertile, moist soil, especially if it is acid, is suitable for this scheme. The site should be in full sun or very light shade.

The main flowering takes place in early summer. Autumn is also a good time, with the vibrant colours of the maples and ginko.

Shrubs
1 *Chamaecyparis obtusa* 'Nana'
2 *Cercidiphyllum japonicum*
3 *Cryptomeria japonica* 'Spiralis'
4 *Ginkgo biloba*
5 *Prunus* × *yedoensis*
6 *Acer palmatum* 'Osakazuki'
7 *Acer palmatum* Dissectum Atropurpureum Group

8 *Acer palmatum* 'Bloodgood'
9 *Azalea* 'Irohayama'
10 *Azalea* 'Hinomayo'
11 *Paeonia suffruticosa*

Climbers
12 *Wisteria sinensis*

Perennials
13 *Alchemilla mollis*
14 *Ophiopogon japonicus*
15 *Iris ensata*

Grasses
16 *Phyllostachys aurea*
17 *Phyllostachys nigra*
18 *Shibatea kumasasa*
19 *Semiarundinaria fastuosa*

Ferns
20 *Dryopteris erythrosora*
21 *Sasa veitchii*

CLASSICAL FORMALITY

WE MAY NOT be able to have the vast acres of Versailles on our doorstep, but traditional formality suits any size of garden and rarely looks out of place. The reliance on form and geometry, rather than colour, means that such gardens are largely unaffected by the seasons and have an atmosphere of calm and deliberation. They are also surprisingly low in maintenance requirements: clipping of evergreens need only be carried out once a year and there are no messy flowers to worry about! Mathematical precision is the watchword if you are serious, so careful planning is required.

Such a garden is an ideal accompaniment to almost any old house, although it can look a bit out of place in front of a humble cottage. The geometric formality also works well with modern buildings, even if the classical urns and symmetry may not.

MAINTENANCE – *Low*

Regular mowing and an annual clipping of the shrubs in late summer are all that is required to keep this garden looking trim. The lavender should be pruned in spring.

SITE AND SEASON

This garden requires sun for most of the day, and is suitable for any reasonably fertile, well-drained soil.

Flowering takes place in late summer, but one of the great things about this style of gardening is that it looks good all year round.

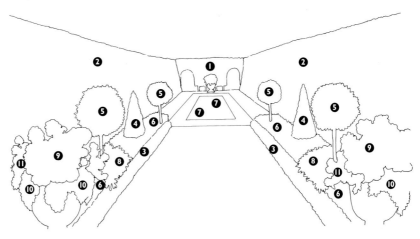

Trees

1 *Carpinus betulus*
2 *Taxus baccata*

Shrubs

3 *Buxus sempervirens* 'Suffruticosa'
4 *Laurus nobilis*

5 *Elaeagnus pungens* 'Maculata'
6 *Lavandula angustifolia* 'Munstead'

Perennials

7 *Nymphaea* 'Attraction'
8 *Penstemon* 'White Bedder'

Half-hardy

9 *Pelargonium* – red zonal variety
10 *Lobelia erinus* 'Sapphire'
11 *Verbena* 'Sissinghurst'

A FOOLPROOF FAMILY GARDEN

HAVEN'T GOT TIME? Hate gardening? This is the planting scheme for you. The selection of plants is designed to provide as much colour and interest through the year as possible, without looking too much like a supermarket car park landscaping; to be as tolerant of a wide range of conditions as it reasonable to ask of plants; and to need as little care as possible. There are cheerful golden-variegated evergreens for the dark depths of winter and long-flowering shrubs and herbaceous plants for the summer. Butterflies will be drawn to the buddleia, providing an extra dimension to the garden and something of interest for children, too. The plants here are all widely available, so there is no need to search out obscure nurseries in order to obtain them.

MAINTENANCE – *Low*

The shrubs, especially the buddleia and lavatera, might need to be cut back if they outgrow their welcome. This should be done straight after flowering and not, as many people do, in the winter. The clematis will flower better if it is cut back by about one-third in late winter. The perennials will need an end-of-year tidy-up.

SITE AND SEASON

This border can be planted in any reasonably fertile soil that receives some sun.

The main flowering season is early summer, although many of the plants will continue to bloom for much longer. For spring interest, bulbs can be planted so that they bloom around and underneath the shrubs.

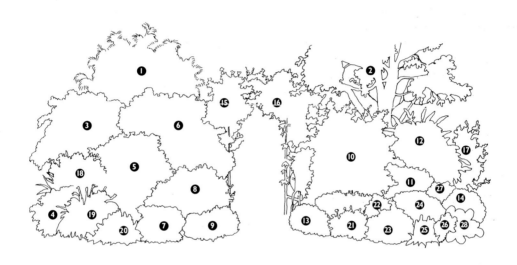

Trees

1 *Sorbus commixta* 'Embley'
2 *Betula jacquemontii*

Shrubs

3 *Genista aetnensis*
4 *Euonymus fortunei* 'Emerald 'n' Gold'
5 *Elaeagnus pungens* 'Maculata'
6 *Corylus avellana* 'Contorta'
7 *Santolina chamaecyparissus*
8 *Hypericum* 'Hidcote'
9 *Erica carnea* 'Westwood Yellow'

10 *Lavatera olbia* 'Rosea'
11 *Potentilla fruticosa* 'Abbotswood'
12 *Buddleia davidii*
13 *Helianthemum* 'Wisley Pink'
14 *Hebe* 'Carl Teschner'

Climbers

15 *Lonicera periclymenum* 'Belgica'
16 *Clematis* 'The President'
17 *Hedera canariensis* 'Gloire de Marengo'

Perennials

18 *Iris sibirica*
19 *Hemerocallis* 'Corky'
20 *Heuchera* var. *diversifolia* 'Palace Purple'
21 *Geum* 'Borisii'
22 *Knautia macedonica*
23 *Geranium* 'Johnson's Blue'
24 *Geranium* 'Claridge Druce'
25 *Stachys byzantina*
26 *Euphorbia dulcis* 'Chameleon'
27 *Achillea millefolium* Summer Pastels Group
28 *Bergenia* 'Silberlicht'

A TOWN GARDEN

SMALL TOWN GARDENS present a real challenge, especially to keen gardeners anxious to grow as wide a range of plants as possible. While there are undoubtedly problems – such as poor, rubble-filled soil and draughts – there are compensations, like the warmth of urban environments and the different microclimates offered by the walls: a warm, sunny wall with a selection of tender species may be only a few metres (yards) away from a shady wall sheltering cool-loving woodlanders. Where soil is thin or non-existent, containers can be used to provide extra planting space, or, as here, to create a miniature pond planted with a pygmy water lily. In a garden with high walls and fences, there may be more vertical than horizontal space; this is ideal for a rich variety of climbers, which will do much to engender the feeling of a green island in the urban desert.

MAINTENANCE – *Low*

None of these plants needs much attention; simply clear up dead stems and leaves in the winter, and prune shrubs after flowering if they begin to exceed the limits of their space (as ceanothus is often wont to do). The roses, if they need pruning, should be cut back by no more than one-third in late winter.

Given that urban soils are often impoverished by the activities of builders, feeding and humus-building are often advisable. An annual application of an organic plant food, plus bucketfuls of compost or manure, can work wonders.

SITE AND SEASON

The house wall in the plan faces the sun, with the bed on each side receiving sun for about half the day. Any reasonably fertile and well-drained soil will do.

The main flowering is in early summer, with continued interest for much of the rest of the year. Bulbs and container-grown half-hardy plants and annuals can be used to extend the season.

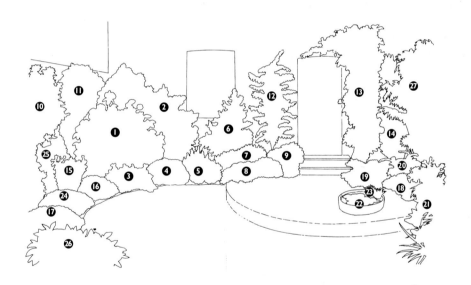

Shrubs

1 *Rosa* 'Louise Odier'
2 *Ceanothus impressus*
3 *Cistus* 'Silver Pink'
4 *Hebe* 'Red Edge'
5 *Rosmarinus officinalis* 'Tuscan Blue'
6 *Leptospermum scoparium* 'Jubilee'
7 *Lavandula stoechas* ssp. *pedunculata*

8 *Helianthemum* 'Wisley Primrose'
9 *Euonymus fortunei* 'Silver Queen'

Climbers

10 *Clematis* 'Richard Pennell'
11 *Jasminum x stephanense*
12 *Abutilon megapotamicum*
13 *Rosa* 'Gloire de Dijon'
14 *Lathyrus latifolius*

Perennials

15 *Campanula persicifolia*
16 *Geranium x oxonianum* 'Winscombe'
17 *Campanula lactiflora* 'Pouffe'
18 *Alchemilla conjuncta*
19 *Campanula garganica*
20 *Dicentra spectabilis*
21 *Hemerocallis* 'Corky'
22 *Nymphaea* 'Pygmaea Alba'

23 *Acorus gramineus* 'Variegatus'
24 *Potentilla recta* 'Warrenii'

Annuals

25 *Lathyrus odoratus* 'Red Ensign'

Grasses

26 *Shibataea kumasasa*
27 *Sinarundinaria nitida*

A GARDEN FOR WILDLIFE

IT IS IMPORTANT that locally native tree, shrub and wildflower species are predominant in wildlife-oriented gardens, so that the insects that are such a vital part of the food chain can find suitable plants on which to feed. Thus the planting here – very much a north-western European one – would have to be modified considerably in other areas. Nevertheless, the wide seasonal range of flowers will feed a very large number of nectar-sucking insects, and the berries borne by shrubs and trees such as *Amelanchier* and *Prunus* will be very popular with birds in winter time. In addition, some annual or biennial plants such as teazel (*Dipsacus fullonum*) and sunflower (*Helianthus annuus*) will provide a larder for seed-eating birds.

Diversity is the key to a good wildlife garden, both of plant species and habitats. It is important to have lots of dense shrubbery in which birds can nest safely, and grass of various lengths for different insects. The cultivation of some species normally considered undesirable is important too: stinging nettles (*Urtica dioica*) are one of the finest food sources for certain butterfly caterpillars.

MAINTENANCE – *Low to very low*

Wildlife gardening suits the lazy gardener, as untidiness is often to the benefit of wildlife: long grass left over winter feeds birds and shelters insects, piles of dead wood provide shelter for invertebrates, and unpruned shrubs provide good nesting and roosting sites. Ideally, a wildlife garden should be managed to provide a balance between being decorative and offering good habitat diversity.

SITE AND SEASON

The species listed are nearly all sun-lovers; if the garden is big enough, some trees could be planted to give more shade. Any well-drained soil, including poor, stony ones and shallow soils over chalk, would be suitable.

The main flowering takes place in midsummer.

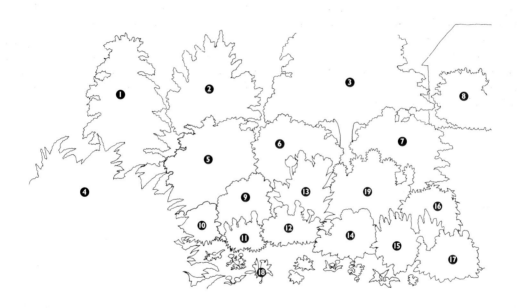

Trees

1 *Juniperus virginiana*
2 *Prunus avium*
3 *Quercus robur*

Shrubs

4 *Buddleia davidii*
5 *Amelanchier × grandiflora*
6 *Viburnum tinus*
7 *Crataegus monogyna*

Climbers

8 *Hedera helix*

Perennials

9 *Tanacetum vulgare*
10 *Knautia arvensis*
11 *Linaria vulgaris*
12 *Centaurea scabiosa*
13 *Dipsacus fullonum*
14 *Sedum spectabile*

15 *Stachys officinalis*
16 *Urtica dioica*
17 *Centranthus ruber*
18 *Hieracium pilosella*

Annuals

19 *Helianthus annuus*

A POND FOR WILDLIFE

EVEN A SMALL POND in the city will attract aquatic insects and probably frogs, appearing as if out of nowhere and illustrating just how important ponds are as part of a strategy for turning a garden into a mini-nature reserve.

The planting around a wildlife pond must reflect the local flora, as many insect species are very specialized feeders. Most of the species illustrated here are from northwestern Europe and a few from North America, with an emphasis on those that can provide for a wide range of wildlife.

Inevitably, given that the needs of people and wildlife are different, the planting will be less colourful than for a strictly ornamental pond, but this should be made up for by the increased interest engendered by visiting birds, insects and amphibians.

With a wildlife pond it is important that there are areas of fairly dense vegetation right down to the water's edge and others where there is just a shallow grass slope, such diversity providing options for the needs of different animals.

MAINTENANCE – *Low*

As with any other pond, dead vegetation will need to be cleared out every year, but this should not be too rigorous, as seedheads will feed the birds and dead vegetation will often shelter insect populations during their hibernation period. Vigorous species can sometimes oust less vigorous ones, in which case some thinning out will be needed. This is most conveniently done in late spring (for one thing, the water is not so cold!).

SITE AND SEASON

The pond will need sunlight for most of the day, although a little shade over one end of it is very beneficial for many aquatic animal species during hot weather. Any reasonably fertile, moisture-holding soil will be suitable.

The main flowering will be in late summer.

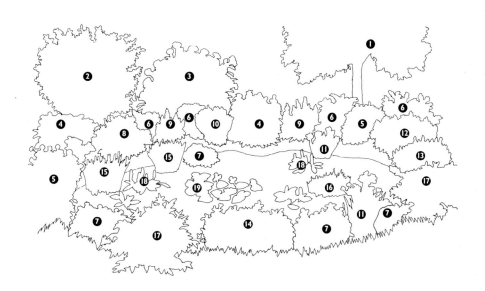

Shrubs
1 *Betula nigra*
2 *Amelanchier lamarckii*

Perennials
3 *Eupatorium purpureum*
4 *Eupatorium cannabinum*
5 *Sanguisorba officinalis*
6 *Filipendula ulmaria*
7 *Mentha aquatica*
8 *Hibiscus moscheutos*

9 *Lobelia cardinalis*
10 *Lythrum salicaria*
11 *Butomus umbellatus*
12 *Lysimachia vulgaris*
13 *Stachys palustris*
14 *Veronica beccabunga*

Grasses
15 *Typha minima*
16 *Schoenoplectus lacustris*
ssp. *tabernaemontani*

Ferns
17 *Osmunda regalis*

Aquatics
18 *Potamogeton nutans*
19 *Nymphoides aquatica*

RHODODENDRON GLORY

O N A N A C I D S O I L , especially a sandy one, rhododendrons, heathers and other related plants thrive. This is just as well, as many other popular garden plants do not do well on these rather poor soils. There is a terrific range of these plants: in the case of rhododendrons, you can have varieties in flower from late winter to midsummer, and heathers all year round.

Selecting the right variety of rhododendron needs care, as many grow far too large for a small or medium-sized garden. Fortunately there are many excellent smaller varieties, and a good number of dwarf species and hybrids that combine well with heathers.

It is not a good idea to rely totally on rhododendrons for colour in the garden, because they finish flowering by midsummer and then tend to look very dark and dull for the rest of the year. Hydrangeas and other acid-tolerant shrubs combine well with them, as do heathers and certain grasses, and will extend the season of interest. Both rhododendrons and heathers have a rather uniform appearance, and the light, airy growth of grasses and sedges can be very welcome among them.

MAINTENANCE – *Very low*

Heathers require a clip back after flowering every other year, but that is about it. Dry years might see some need for watering, and if drought is a problem, mulching areas of bare earth with chipped bark is advisable.

SITE AND SEASON

Any soil on the acid side of neutral is suitable, especially those that are peaty or sandy. This planting requires full sun, with the exception of the plants on the far right, which prefer a little shade. The rhododendrons are all tolerant of some light shade, but the heathers are not.

The flowering season for this scheme is from late spring to early summer.

Trees
1 *Parrotia persica*
2 *Nyssa sylvatica*

Shrubs
3 *Erica arborea* var. *alpina*
4 *Rhododendron* 'Pink Pearl'
5 *Kalmia latifolia*
6 *Rhododendron augustinii*
7 *Rhododendron* 'Sappho'
8 *Fothergilla gardenii* Monticola Group
9 *Rhododendron* 'Palestrina'
10 *Rhododendron* Elizabeth Group

11 *Rhododendron yakushimanum*
12 *Rhododendron luteum*
13 *Rhododendron* 'Unique'
14 *Erica* x *veitchii* 'Exeter'
15 *Genista pilosa* 'Procumbens'
16 *Calluna vulgaris* 'Boskoop'
17 *Phyllodoce empetriformis*
18 *Andromeda polifolia*

Bulbs
19 *Hyacinthoides non-scriptus*

Grasses
20 *Festuca ovina* 'Glauca'
21 *Carex buchananii*
22 *Molinia caerulea* 'Variegata'
23 *Deschampsia flexuosa* 'Tatra Gold'

A SHELTERED SITE

WALLS THAT FACE THE SUN, are protected from cold winds and have good frost drainage are an absolute boon to gardeners. They provide the kind of warm microclimate that is ideal for tender plants, protecting them from the worst of the winter cold and enhancing the effect of summer heat. Exotic foliage plants, like the large-leaved magnolias and *Melianthus major*, are in their element and can form the basis of such a planting. Combine them with showy, free-flowering shrubs like abutilons to make a truly unusual planting. Of course, there is a risk that an unusually hard winter will kill off all your efforts, but this can be avoided to some extent if the roots and lower parts of the plants are protected by insulating materials such as straw (see page 15). Fortunately, many of the plants in this border are quick growing and are thus well able to spring up again from the base. They are also easy to propagate. Cuttings can be taken from early summer onwards and overwintered under cover. Some of these can be distributed to gardening friends, an apparently selfless activity but really a disguised way of protecting your assets, since you can always ask for cuttings in return if you lose your plants.

MAINTENANCE – *Low to medium*

The main tasks here are protecting the plants in winter, and pruning. Many of these are vigorous, almost rampant growers and so require frequent cutting back. This is best done after the winter, as the more growth that is left on them, the better the plants will survive inclement weather.

SITE AND SEASON

A warm and sheltered site receiving as much sun as possible is essential for this scheme. A well-drained soil is also important, but fertility is not; indeed, it could be argued that these plants will survive cold winters better on poor soil.

Most of the plants flower in early summer. Many will bloom again later in the year, and abutilons are capable of flowering all year round if the winter is mild. For colour later in the year, the bright American salvias such as the pineapple sage (*Salvia rutilans*) can be added.

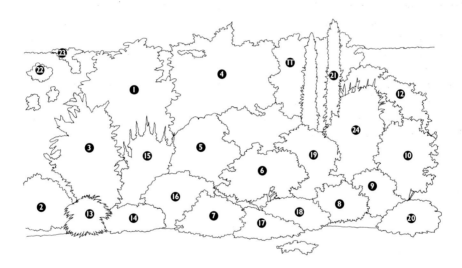

Trees

1 *Magnolia delavayi*

Shrubs

2 *Myrtus communis* ssp. *tarentina*
3 *Callistemon rigidus*
4 *Rosa banksiae* 'Lutea'
5 *Clianthus puniceus*
6 *Rhododendron* × *fragrantissimum*
7 *Convolvulus cneorum*
8 *Aloysia citriodora*
9 *Correa* 'Mannii'
10 *Abutilon* 'Canary Bird'

Climbers

11 *Solanum jasminoides* 'Album'
12 *Clematis florida* 'Sieboldii'

Perennials

13 *Fascicularia pitcairniifolia*
14 *Diascia cordata*
15 *Salvia guaranitica*
16 *Mimulus aurantiacus*
17 *Convolvulus althaeoides*
18 *Geranium palmatum*
19 *Melianthus major*
20 *Malvastrum lateritium*
21 *Echium pininana*

22 *Lampranthus spectabilis* 'Tresco Apricot'
23 *Lampranthus spectabilis* 'Tresco Red'

Grasses

24 *Arundo donax* 'Variegata'

A SCHEME FOR FULL SHADE

AREAS OF FULL SHADE, where there is no direct sunlight, can be surprisingly colourful in spring with the flowers of primulas, pulmonarias, bulbs and other woodland plants. Some bulbous and tuberous plants, such as anemones, trilliums and erythroniums, are summer dormant, so they disappear underground after flowering. This means that the role of foliage plants is very important for interest in the summer. Fortunately, there is a wide variety of ferns and evergreen plants for situations like this, such as the bugle (*Ajuga reptans*) so that, with imagination, a shaded part of the garden can look good for most of the year.

Shade-tolerant shrubs tend to be evergreen with glossy, dark green leaves – a rather depressing prospect in reduced-light conditions. Luckily, however, there are a few excellent and easy-to-grow variegated shrubs that will serve to light up the gloom.

MAINTENANCE – Low

Shade does not encourage many weeds, and shade-loving plants do not make a lot of growth, so all in all not much maintenance is required. Leaf-fall from trees in the autumn can smother plants underneath, especially evergreens, so clearing up leaves is important. Since leaf-derived humus is very beneficial for many plants from woodland environments, and shady areas in gardens are often short of it, the collected leaves should be made into compost for later use as a mulch. Alternatively, they can be shredded and applied around the plants as a mulch without composting.

SITE AND SEASON

Any reasonably fertile, well-drained soil with average moisture would be suitable for this scheme. 'Full shade' is where there is little direct sunlight, but without being dark.

Flowering will be in late spring, with foliage interest for much of the year. The pulmonarias are invaluable for their long season of interest.

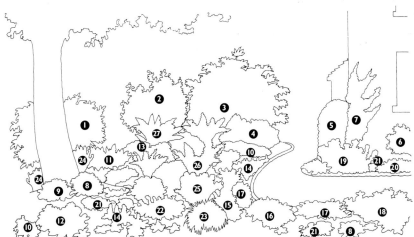

Shrubs
1 *Prunus lusitanica*
2 *Elaeagnus × ebbingei* 'Gilt Edge'
3 *Fatsia japonica*
4 *Euonymus fortunei* 'Variegatus'
5 *Buxus sempervirens*
6 *Daphne mezereum*

Climbers
7 *Hedera helix* 'Glacier'

Perennials
8 *Primula vulgaris*
9 *Viola odorata*
10 *Galium odoratum*
11 *Convallaria majalis*
12 *Pulmonaria rubra*
13 *Trillium grandiflorum*
14 *Ajuga reptans* 'Jungle Beauty'
15 *Mertensia pulmonarioides*
16 *Lamium maculatum*
17 *Asarum europaeum*
18 *Lamium argentatum*
19 *Euphorbia robbiae*
20 *Pulmonaria saccharata*

Bulbs
21 *Anemone blanda*
22 *Erythronium dens-canis*

Grasses
23 *Carex oshimensis* 'Evergold'

Ferns
24 *Asplenium scolopendrium*
25 *Athyrium felix-femina*
26 *Dryopteris affinis*
27 *Matteuccia struthiopteris*

A COTTAGE GARDEN IN LIGHT SHADE

THE FASHIONABLE cottage garden of today bears little resemblance to the plots that our ancestors would have had – utilitarian rows of vegetables with a few herbs and the occasional flower – but these humble origins have inspired an important garden movement of relaxed planting with a variety of shrubs, perennials and annuals. Allowing plants to self-seed, as with the foxgloves (*Digitalis purpurea*) here, is an important part of the philosophy: it lets the plants themselves participate in the design, choosing their own place in which to grow.

MAINTENANCE – Low

The perennials will need only an annual cutting back, either after flowering if you value a tidy garden, or at the end of the year if you are not too worried. An advantage of not cutting back the foxgloves and the campanula is that they both self-seed freely, spreading the group and sending up odd plants elsewhere, but never enough to become a nuisance. All the perennials here will live for many years with no other maintenance.

SITE AND SEASON

Any well-drained, reasonably fertile soil is suitable for this scheme, although it should preferably be slightly acid, and certainly not dry. The site should receive sun for no more than half the day, or dappled sunlight all day.

The flowering season is from early to midsummer, with some year-long foliage interest. The camellia and pulmonaria are spring flowering, while the mahonia blooms in winter.

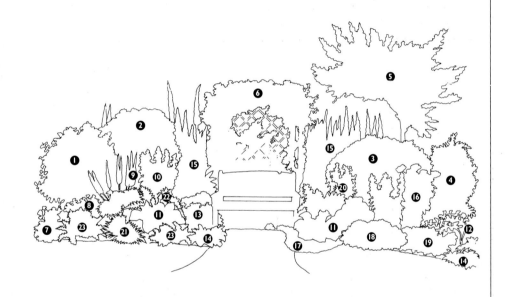

Shrubs
1 *Camellia* × *williamsii* 'Donation'
2 *Hydrangea macrophylla* 'Blue Wave'
3 *Rubus* 'Benenden'
4 *Mahonia* × *media* 'Charity'
5 *Cornus kousa* var. *chinensis*

Climbers
6 *Lonicera periclymenum* 'Belgica'

Perennials
7 *Meconopsis cambrica*
8 *Astrantia major*
9 *Ligularia przewalskii*
10 *Campanula latifolia* var. *macrantha*
11 *Hosta sieboldiana*
12 *Polygonatum* × *hybridum*
13 *Primula florindae*
14 *Pulmonaria saccharata*
15 *Digitalis purpurea*
16 *Phlox paniculata*
17 *Phlox stolonifera*
18 *Geranium endressii*
19 *Pachysandra terminalis*

Bulbs
20 *Lilium martagon*

Grasses
21 *Milium effusum* 'Aureum'

Ferns
22 *Dryopteris dilatata*
23 *Polypodium vulgare*

A HOT, DRY CLIMATE

GARDENS IN CLIMATES that have hot, dry summers are often at their best in spring and autumn, many of the plants becoming more or less dormant in summer in order to conserve moisture.

Selecting plants that are drought tolerant will drastically reduce the amount of water needed for irrigation, and consequently the cost and labour involved in garden maintenance. These plants can also help to reduce the fire risk that is ever-present in these regions. Fortunately many new dry-land species are coming on to the market, a lot of them natives of California, South Africa or Australia, so the choice of plants is improving rapidly.

Most of the plants in this scheme are evergreen, often with very attractive greyish foliage; this should be made a feature, as there may be few flowers during the summer. In the very driest areas cacti and succulents, such as agaves and aloes, can be grown for contrast.

Bulbs have a special place in dry gardens, flowering during the winter and early spring, and then dying down as the sun rises to its summer height. Species tulips are among the most colourful, reliable and easily available. During the hot season, annuals are often the best bet for colour if a small area can be kept irrigated for them. Indeed, dry-land annuals give us the most intensely coloured of all flowers.

MAINTENANCE – Low

In hot, dry climates relatively little growth is made, and consequently the need for pruning or clearing up will be minimal. The plants selected are all drought tolerant, so irrigation is not necessary once they are established. In the early years, however, water will be needed; it should be given infrequently and in sufficient quantity to soak the soil thoroughly – 'little and often' is a recipe for disaster.

SITE AND SEASON

This scheme is suitable for a site in full sun or light shade, and any soil that is not seriously and seasonally waterlogged.

The main flowering is in late spring, although flowering times may vary greatly in different regions. Bulbs can be grown for earlier colour and annuals for later.

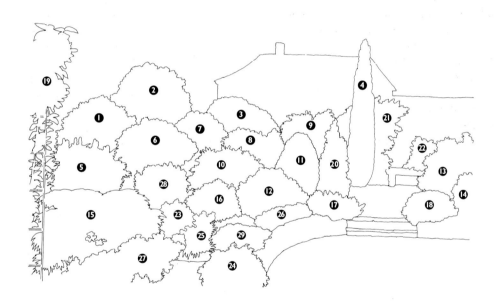

Trees

1 *Feijoa sellowiana*
2 *Arbutus unedo*
3 *Acacia dealbata*
4 *Cupressus sempervirens*

Shrubs

5 *Banksia spinulosa*
6 *Dendromecon rigida*
7 *Caesalpinia gilliesii*
8 *Banksia speciosa*
9 *Callistemon citrinus*

10 *Mahonia* 'Golden Abundance'
11 *Dodonaea viscosa* 'Purpurea'
12 *Cistus × purpureus*
13 *Nerium oleander* 'Tito Poggi'
14 *Grevillea rosmarinifolia*

Dwarf shrubs/ground cover

15 *Juniperus × media* 'Pfitzeriana'

16 *Banksia dryandroides*
17 *Banksia blechnifolia*
18 *Cistus salviifolius*

Climbers

19 *Pyrostegia venusta*
20 *Sollya heterophylla*
21 *Bougainvillea spectabilis*
22 *Plumbago auriculata*

Perennials

23 *Penstemon eatonii*
24 *Zauschneria californica*

Bulbs

25 *Freesia* 'Yellow River'
26 *Tulipa tarda*

Annuals/biennials

27 *Eschscholzia californica*
28 *Oenothera hookeri*
29 *Nemophila menziesii*

A COLD GARDEN

Not many plants will survive tempera-tures as low as -40°C (-4°F, US zone 3) but these will, with some to as low as -45°C (-13°F, US zone 2). As a general rule, herbaceous plants, which can retreat below ground, are hardier than woody plants, which have to take the full force of arctic winds. The perennials' high rate of growth enables them to take maximum advantage of short growing seasons, especially when the day-length is long at high latitudes. Among evergreens, only the hardier conifers will survive, others becoming hopelessly wind burned and dehydrated. When

you are selecting plants for cold places it always helps to discover their region of origin, those from northern and north-eastern America and Asia being the toughest, although there are surprises, such as the oriental poppy (*Papaver orientale*) from Turkey.

In addition to these plants, many of the prairie plants given on pages 82–3 will thrive in these con-ditions. Annuals can also be used to provide summer colour, although many may have to be started off under cover.

MAINTENANCE – *Low to medium*

Since most of these are robust herbaceous plants, they will need only an end-of-year tidy-up. If the shrubs require pruning, this should be carried out just after flowering.

SITE AND SEASON

Plant up this border in full sun and any reasonably fertile, well-drained soil.

The main season of interest is early summer, although it should be noted that many plants flower later in cold climates. For later colour, North American prairie perennials, such as rudbeckias and golden rods, can be used as border plants for this scheme.

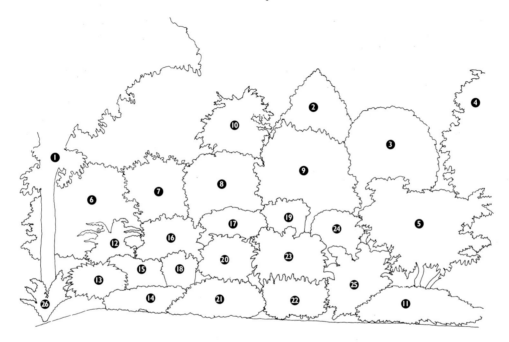

Trees

1 *Betula papyrifera*
2 *Picea glauca*
3 *Malus × schiedeckeri* 'Red Jade'
4 *Acer saccharum*
5 *Rhus typhina* 'Laciniata'

Shrubs

6 *Spiraea × vanhouttei*
7 *Cornus alba* 'Elegantissima'
8 *Rosa rugosa*
9 *Syringa vulgaris* 'Madame Antoine Buchner'

10 *Hippophae rhamnoides*
11 *Juniperus horizontalis* 'Wiltonii'

Perennials

12 *Dicentra spectabilis*
13 *Hosta plantaginea*
14 *Geranium sanguineum*
15 *Alchemilla mollis*
16 *Hemerocallis lilioasphodelus*
17 *Achillea* 'Moonshine'
18 *Allium caeruleum*

19 *Iris sibirica* 'Perry's Blue'
20 *Lysimachia clethroides*
21 *Nepeta × faassenii*
22 *Veronica incana*
23 *Paeonia lactiflora* 'Sarah Bernhardt'
24 *Saponaria officinalis*
25 *Papaver orientale* 'Turkish Delight'

Ferns

26 *Polystichium acrostichoides*

A PRAIRIE GARDEN

THE AMERICAN PRAIRIE can be likened to a wildflower meadow on a huge scale, with an enormous and colourful variety of plant life, much of it majestic in scale, with some of the grasses and wildflowers growing to more than 2m (6ft) tall. Prairie gardens have been increasing in popularity, and not just in North America, because – like wildflower meadows – they require little maintenance once they are established. The vigour of prairie plants makes them especially suitable for areas where the soil is very fertile, because they can resist the encroachment of the strong-growing grasses that tend to make growing wildflowers difficult on these soils.

Prairie gardens are very wildlife friendly, providing good cover and a rich food resource for a wide variety of insects, birds and mammals. Late summer and early autumn are when prairie wildflowers are at their most colourful and most attractive to butterflies. If uncut, the seedheads of the grasses and perennials will help to feed birds throughout the winter.

MAINTENANCE – *Low to very low*

Once established, a prairie garden needs only an annual cut back, preferably in late winter, although if tidiness is important this can be done in late autumn. Over time, some species may come to dominate, in which case the more aggressive ones can be thinned out.

SITE AND SEASON

This garden requires full sun and any reasonably well-drained, fertile soil. It is especially suitable for rich terrain.

Late summer is the main flowering season, although a good mix of prairie wildflowers will provide colour from spring until late autumn.

Perennials

1 *Asclepias tuberosa*
2 *Baptisia leucantha*
3 *Desmodium canadense*
4 *Liatris aspera*
5 *Helianthus × laetiflorus*
6 *Ratabida pinnata*
7 *Rudbeckia subtomentosa*
8 *Silphium laciniatum*
9 *Solidago speciosa*
10 *Veronicastrum virginicum*
11 *Eupatorium purpureum* ssp. *maculatum*
12 *Vernonia fasciculata*
13 *Euphorbia corollata*
14 *Filipendula rubra*
15 *Rudbeckia hirta*
16 *Eryngium yuccifolium*

Grasses

17 *Andropogon gerardii*
18 *Panicum virgatum*
19 *Sorghastrum nutans*
20 *Sporobolus heterolepis*

A COASTAL GARDEN

THE SEASIDE may be a fine place for a holiday, but it is a difficult one in which to garden – we can flee indoors from storms, but plants cannot. However, plants that are adapted to life by the coast are often very good looking, and the waxy grey leaves and stems that are their means of protection from harsh, salt-laden winds are an attractive feature. Most are also evergreen, an additional advantage. Many coastal plants, or those that come from similar harsh environments, also have a distinctive foliage form, such as the rosettes of yuccas and cordylines. Given such a range of interesting foliage, the possibilities for creating a garden are excellent, even before flowers are considered. As a general rule, most grey-leaved plants and those with leathery leaves are suitable for coastal planting.

A good windbreak is a must for any seaside garden. Behind this it is possible to make use of the relatively warm winter temperatures typical of the coast. The sycamore (*Acer pseudoplatanus*) is one of the best windbreaks, but the pine used here is better looking and also fast growing.

MAINTENANCE – Low

Most of these plants are shrubby and hence do not need much of an annual tidy-up. Coastal soils are often thin and the environment is very drying, so watering may have to be considered in summer, and any bare areas of soil should be mulched. *Hippophae rhamnoides* has a tendency to sucker, so an eye should be kept out for growths around it that might displace neighbouring plants. Some of the larger shrubs may need occasional pruning.

SITE AND SEASON

Any well-drained soil is suitable for this scheme, including a poor, dry, stony one. Full sun, however, is essential.

The main flowering takes place in midsummer, although the foliage in the border looks attractive all year round. Bulbs can be planted in more sheltered areas for spring colour. Small rockery plants, which also tend to be spring flowering, could also be used.

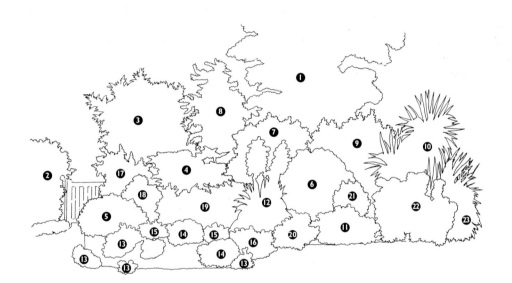

Trees
1 *Pinus radiata*

Shrubs
2 *Escallonia rubra* var. *macrantha*
3 *Tamarix ramosissima*
4 *Fuchsia magellanica* 'Riccartonii'
5 *Hebe* x *franciscana* 'Blue Gem'
6 *Rosa pimpinellifolia*

7 *Berberis darwinii*
8 *Hippophae rhamnoides*
9 *Elaeagnus commutata*
10 *Cordyline australis*
11 *Brachyglottis rotundifolia*
12 *Yucca filamentosa*

Perennials
13 *Armeria maritima*
14 *Dianthus caesius*
15 *Mertensia maritima*
16 *Gaillardia pulchella*

17 *Althaea officinalis*
18 *Eryngium planum*
19 *Limonium latifolium*
20 *Oenothera odorata* 'Sulphurea'
21 *Phygelius capensis* var. *coccineus*
22 *Euphorbia characias*

Grasses
23 *Elymus arenarius*

HEATHLAND COLOUR

CHARACTERIZED by poor, acid soil and strong winds, heathland can seem an inhospitable place for a garden. Yet heathland plants, notably the heathers (*Calluna*, *Daboecia* and *Erica* varieties), can be very colourful, and have a very long flowering season. Birches (*Betula* species) and sorbus provide some shelter and are used to create the basic structure of this garden, while the ground can be covered with a variety of heathers to flower all year long, but with perhaps the widest range of varieties blooming in late summer. The smaller 'whipcord' hebes, superficially like heathers but less attractive in flower, also thrive on heathland, although most do best in areas swept by warm, moist winds rather than cold ones, while the pernettyas have coloured berries that last well. Alternatively, dwarf rhododendrons might be combined with the heathers and allowed to spread to form a tight, weed-excluding mass of vegetation.

MAINTENANCE – *Low to very low*

Beyond clipping some of the more straggly heather growths every other year after flowering, this planting requires little maintenance. Weeds must be rigorously removed in the first few years, but after this the plants should mesh together to exclude them.

SITE AND SEASON

The soil needs to be acid and fairly well drained in order for these plants to thrive, although it can be quite poor. The planting is suitable for windswept sites in full sun, although in warmer areas *Gentiana sino-ornata* will need shade.

Flowering takes place from late summer to early autumn. Other varieties of heather, hebe and related plants may be added to create a planting that will be colourful all year long.

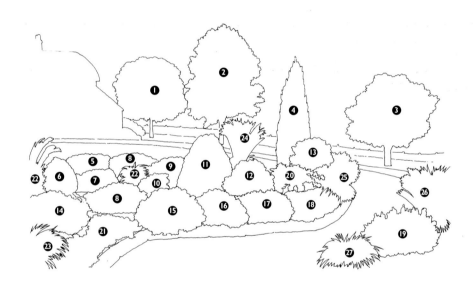

Trees

1 *Sorbus vilmorinii*
2 *Betula jacquemontii*
3 *Sorbus hupehensis*

Shrubs

4 *Juniperus scopulorum* 'Skyrocket'
5 *Calluna vulgaris* 'Multi-colour'
6 *Hebe cupressoides*
7 *Erica vagans* 'Lyonesse'
8 *Erica cinerea* 'Purple Beauty'
9 *Erica tetralix* 'Pink Star'
10 *Erica cinerea* 'Romiley'
11 *Picea glauca* var. *albertiana* 'Conica'
12 *Gaultheria mucronata* 'Bell's Seedling'
13 *Gaultheria mucronata* 'Alba'
14 *Erica tetralix* 'Alba Mollis'
15 *Hebe* 'Autumn Glory'
16 *Daboecia cantabrica* 'Bicolor'
17 *Calluna vulgaris* 'Elsie Purnell'
18 *Erica carnea* 'Springwood White'
19 *Erica vagans* 'Birch Glow'

Perennials

20 *Gentiana asclepiadea*
21 *Gentiana sino-ornata*

Grasses

22 *Carex testacea*
23 *Carex comans* bronze
24 *Molinia caerulea* 'Winter-feuer'
25 *Deschampsia cespitosa* 'Bronzeschleier'
26 *Molinia caerulea* 'Windspiel'
27 *Uncinia rubra*

FLOWERS AND FOLIAGE FOR WETLAND

THIS PLANTING is for an area of badly drained land, where low maintenance is a priority and vigorous perennials that can look after themselves are needed. It is designed to make the most of plants with attractive foliage as well as flowers.

Petasites is one of the largest leaved of all perennials, and looks magnificently exotic, as will the macleaya once it has had a chance to get established. They and the spartina are best used as background for the smaller and more colourful astilbes and primulas. Both of these plants are available in a great many colours and varieties, and on damp ground where there is no competition they will spread to form sizable clumps. The bulb camassia naturalizes easily, seeding itself around, and the ferns will naturalize too, although the blechnum is suitable only for areas that do not experience hard winters. It should be noted that the petasites and spartina are very invasive – ideal for the larger garden, but perhaps not so welcome in smaller ones!

MAINTENANCE – Low to very low

This is designed as a low-maintenance planting, with robust varieties that will spread with little intervention. However, it is important that the site is as weed free as possible before planting, and that it is kept this way during the first two years as the plants become established. Routine maintenance is restricted to an annual end-of-year clear-up of dead growth, but even this is not strictly necessary. In colder areas where the blechnum fern is not evergreen, it will appreciate a covering of straw or similar material as protection against hard frosts.

SITE AND SEASON

Midsummer, with flowering of many plants until early autumn and a long season of foliage interest.

Partial shade suits the majority of these plants best, full sun is suitable so long as the soil remains moist through the summer. The soil needs to be reasonably fertile.

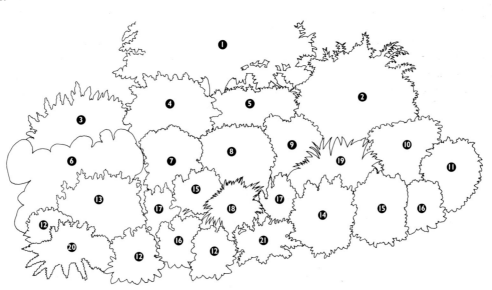

Trees

1 *Pterocarya fraxinifolia*
2 *Salix alba vitellina* 'Britzensis'

Shrubs

3 *Clethra alnifolia* 'Paniculata'
4 *Sorbaria arborea*
5 *Salix exigua*

Perennials

6 *Petasites japonicus* var. *giganteus*

7 *Thalictrum delavayi*
8 *Macleaya cordata*
9 *Filipendula purpurea*
10 *Aruncus dioicus* 'Kneiffii'
11 *Astilbe* 'Straussenfeder'
12 *Primula pulverulenta*
13 *Astilbe* 'Venus'
14 *Astilbe* 'Irrlicht'
15 *Astilbe* 'Fanal'
16 *Primula japonica* 'Postford White'

Bulbs

17 *Camassia esculenta*

Grasses

18 *Carex elata* 'Aurea'
19 *Spartina pectinata* 'Aureomarginata'

Ferns

20 *Blechnum chilense*
21 *Onoclea sensibilis*

A GARDEN FOR A WHEELCHAIR USER

RAISED BEDS, sinks, troughs and plants in pots on shelves bring the garden to a height at which it is possible for the wheelchair-bound to enjoy them. Alpines, dwarf conifers, dwarf bulbs and other small plants are eminently suitable for this kind of gardening, and have the advantage that a lot of variety can be packed into a small space. Gardening in containers and raised beds also means that close attention can be given to catering for the needs of individual plants, and different composts can be used. Raised beds and containers for lime-loving and lime-hating plants will have to be planned carefully so that they are all within reach from the wheelchair.

MAINTENANCE – *Medium*

The level of maintenance can be geared closely to the needs of the individual. Most of the plants require little care, although weeding of alpines has to be rigorous. The keen disabled gardener will probably want plenty to do, in which case the more challenging alpines, such as the auriculas, will provide plenty of interest. Alternatively, space in a raised bed with at least 30cm (12in) of root depth could be given over to the cultivation of annuals and vegetables, such as salad crops.

SITE AND SEASON

This garden requires full sun for as much of the day as possible, although the lime-hating plants in the raised bed on the left will appreciate some shade for a few hours each day. These are also very intolerant of drying out, and need a humus-rich, lime-free soil. The other plants require a free-draining, gritty soil.

The main flowering is in mid-spring. Further dwarf bulbs can be added for earlier interest, and other alpines used for colour until autumn.

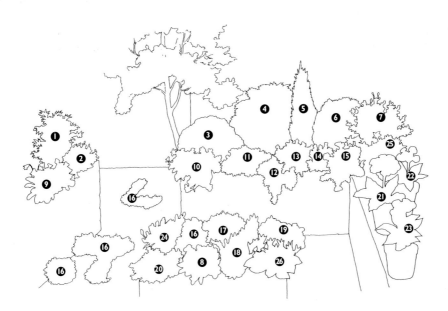

Dwarf trees and shrubs

1 *Andromeda polifolia* 'Compacta'
2 *Cassiope* 'Edinburgh'
3 *Picea mariana* 'Nana'
4 *Chamaecyparis pisifera* 'Filifera Aurea'
5 *Juniperus communis* 'Hibernica'
6 *Pinus heldreichii* 'Schmidtii'
7 *Salix helvetica*
8 *Salix reticulata*

Perennials

9 *Shortia galacifolia*
10 *Viola* 'Jackanapes'
11 *Armeria juniperifolia*
12 *Saxifraga* 'Tumbling Waters'
13 *Tanacetum densum* ssp. *amani*
14 *Saxifraga sempervivum*
15 *Euphorbia myrsinites*
16 *Primula hirsuta*
17 *Erinus alpinus*
18 *Helichrysum coralloides*

19 *Saxifraga oppositifolia*
20 *Gentiana verna*
21 *Primula auricula* 'Chloe'
22 *Primula auricula* 'Janie Hill'
23 *Primula auricula* 'Mark'

Bulbs

24 *Muscari aucheri*
25 *Tulipa tarda*
26 *Cyclamen repandum*

THREE WINDOWBOXES

WINDOWBOXES CAN MAKE all the difference to a house, whether you have a garden or not. Plants will need to be chosen carefully for the aspect: a sunny windowsill is ideal for a traditional mix of pelargoniums and annuals, but shade-tolerant alpines and ferns would be more appropriate for a window that receives no sun. Civic pride often demands a spectacular summer display of pelargoniums and other summer flowers, but this is quite hard work, as frequent watering and feeding are vital for success. Alpines are especially suitable for windowboxes, because of their small size and tolerance of climatic extremes; many also flower in early spring or even late winter. Using alpines and dwarf bulbs can mean that a windowbox is more or less permanent, as they will not outgrow the container for many years. Heathers and small hebes are also deservedly popular as permanent plantings, but need to be kept carefully pruned every year or they will begin to look straggly. If clipping is no problem, then the adventurous might even want to try their hand with a little miniature topiary; the dwarf box, *Buxus sempervirens* 'Suffruticosa' is ideal.

MAINTENANCE – *Medium*

Like all containers, windowboxes need daily watering in dry conditions. Permanently planted boxes should be fed regularly throughout the growing season, and this is best done through the application of a slow-release fertilizer in spring. Summer windowboxes planted with annuals and half-hardy perennials benefit from generous and regular feeding; these are greedy plants and there will probably not be enough nutrients in the compost to keep them in good condition all summer. Dwarf shrubs like heathers should be cut back after flowering, but alpines require very little care.

SITE AND SEASON

Scheme 1 needs a well-drained, low-lime compost, scheme 2 a high-nutrient compost, and scheme 3 a gritty but not especially rich mixture.

Sun is required for most of the day for schemes 1 and 2. Scheme 3 should receive sun for no more than half the day.

1 PERMANENT, SHOWN IN EARLY SPRING

Dwarf shrubs
1 *Calluna vulgaris* 'Aurea'
2 *Erica carnea* 'Springwood Pink'

Perennials
3 *Dianthus* 'Little Jock'

Bulbs
4 *Crocus chrysanthus* 'E.A. Bowles'
5 *Galanthus nivalis*
6 *Crocus chrysanthus* 'Blue Pearl'

2 SEASONAL, SHOWN IN SUMMER

Annual
1 *Lobularia maritima* 'Little Dorrit'

Half-hardy
2 *Pelargonium* 'Balcon Rouge'
3 *Chlorophytum comosum* 'Vittatum'
4 *Pelargonium* 'Balcon Rose'
5 *Lotus berthelotii*
6 *Nierembergia caerulea*

3 PERMANENT/ALPINE, SHOWN IN EARLY SPRING

Dwarf shrub
1 *Salix reticulata*

Perennials
2 *Campanula* 'Joe Elliott'
3 *Saxifraga* 'Jenkinsiae'
4 *Saxifraga* × *apiculata*
5 *Asperula suberosa*
6 *Saxifraga oppositifolia*
7 *Armeria juniperifolia*

Author's acknowledgements

This book is the product of years of garden visiting in many countries and innumerable discussions with other gardeners and designers. I am very grateful to those people who have generously allowed me access to their gardens and taken the time to discuss them with me. It is quite impossible to list them all, but the following I think deserve special thanks for teaching me, inspiring me, offering me hospitality or unlocking the doors of secret gardens to me: in Brazil, Conrad Hamerman and the late Roberto Burle Marx; in Germany, Urs Walser and Hans Simon; in The Netherlands, Piet and Anja Oudolf, Leo den Dulk and Rob Leopold; and in Britain, Nori and Sandra Pope of Hadspen House and Guy Acloques of Alderley Grange, and, for their frequent hospitality in London, Helen and Johnathan Barnes. I would also like to say thank you to Sharron Long, who read the manuscript and helped with research, to my wonderful agent Fiona Lindsay, and to my partner Jo Eliot, for her constant love and support.

Photographic acknowledgements

Andrew Lawson 2 (Ashtree Cottage, Wilts), 7 (Ashtree Cottage, Wilts), 11, 13, 14–15 (Alderley Grange, Glos), 16 (The Priory, Kemerton, Worcs), 21, 24–25 (Ashtree, Cottage, Wilts), 30 (The Manor House, Upton Grey, Wilts), 33 left, 33 right, 36, (Beth Chatto Gardens, Essex), 36–37 (Eastgrove Cottage, Worcs), 38–39 (Barnsley House, Glos); **Noël Kingsbury** 9 (Frau Bahlo, Fürth im Odenwald), 29 (Westpark, Münich/Designer: Rosemary Weisse); **Piet Oudolf** 34–35.

Index